Urban Fiscal Stress

Urban Fiscal Stress

A Comparative Analysis of 66 U.S. Cities

James M. Howell
The First National Bank
of Boston

Charles F. Stamm
Touche Ross & Co.

LexingtonBooks
D.C. Heath and Company
Lexington, Massachusetts
Toronto

Library of Congress Cataloging in Publication Data

Boston. First National Bank. Economics Dept. Urban fiscal stress.

"Undertaken jointly by the Economics Department of the First National Bank of Boston and Touche Ross & Co."
Includes index.
1. Municipal finance—United States—Case studies. I. Howell, James M. II. Stamm, Charles F. III. Touche Ross & Co. IV. Title.
HJ9145   1979a   336.73   79-3083
ISBN 0-669-03372-3

Published simultaneously in Canada.

Printed in the United States of America.

International Standard Book Number: 0-669-03372-3.

Library of Congress Catalog Card Number: 79-3083.

Contents

7034115

List of Figures and Tables

Foreword

Urban Fiscal Stress: A Comparative Analysis of 66 U.S. Cities is a welcome addition to the national debate over the condition of our cities. The book's analysis provides important information and insights into a subject which deserves far more attention than it has received.

Indeed, for almost a decade, the issue of whether or not our cities are in crisis has been almost studiously ignored. No genuine urban policies appeared in the 1970s and the fledgling ones that emerged in the 1960s were declared failures before they were scarcely in place. In recent years, the academic world, in particular, has been quick to declare that whatever problems existed in cities were inevitable. At the same time, through programs such as General Revenue Sharing, the role of the Federal Government increasingly has been to "drop the money and run."

It is illuminating that the debate about the future of the nation's urban areas is raised in *Urban Fiscal Stress*—not by academicians or policymakers—but by professionals from the private sector. The study represents responsible and well-researched analysis, employing sophisticated methodologies.

The overwhelming conclusion that emerges from *Urban Fiscal Stress* is a persuasive critique of conventional wisdom—that our older industrialized cities are irrevocably doomed. In fact, according to the analysis, they are considerably better off financially than we have generally assumed. Moreover, the fiscal capacity of our cities to provide services does not seem necessarily determined by their social and economic conditions alone; effective management may well make the difference between stress and stability. In short, with appropriate national and state urban policies geared to their situations, cities have the capacity to direct their own destinies.

Findings such as these are certain to provoke angry reactions from the right and the left. From the right, the prospect of any new national and state urban policies is sure to be unsettling. From the left, it will be disconcerting to learn that the grand designs which might have been appropriate in the fifties and sixties—the Urban Renewal, Community Action, and Model Cities programs—no longer fit urban realities.

For someone who has followed the course of urban events for a quarter of a century, the fresh look at urban conditions that *Urban Fiscal Stress* provides is particularly useful. The 1980s are not the fifties and sixties, and the greatest mistake policymakers at every level can make is to continue as if they were.

Almost ten years ago, I gave a series of lectures at Columbia University on the urban crisis entitled "The Necessary Majority." In examining the urban situation at that time, I offered two partial explanations, one of which was "the mismatch between the character of the problems involved and the nature of the responses devised." *Urban Fiscal Stress* goes to the heart of this mismatch, by clearly delineating the differences between social, economic, structural, and fiscal problems and suggesting that different policies and different criteria for distributing funds are required for different problems. The special strength of this book is that it gives us improved techniques for developing policies and distributing funds, even as new problems emerge on the urban scene.

Looking ahead to the eighties at least three new forces will condition the urban community: energy, environment, and the cost of land; particularly suburban land. The energy crisis offers a potential both for jobs and households in densely settled older communities. Increased attention to the environment not only places constraints on suburban sprawl and piecemeal development, but also provides a new emphasis on rehabilitation and renewal within older cities. Most of all, the spiraling costs of land—in a nation with no genuine land policy—will continue to influence the future course of cities. Rapidly rising land values are at the root of some of the local fiscal issues that prompted Proposition 13 and its counterparts across the country.

The implications of these and other developments for urban fiscal management are well-documented in *Urban Fiscal Stress*. Perhaps most important of all is the urgent review of public policy that the book recommends. At rock bottom, the conclusion I have drawn from the analysis is that we should be talking about urban options rather than urban crises, for the vast majority of cities studied are in relatively good financial shape. Even in the fiscally stressed cities—that is where tax, spending, and debt are well beyond that of cities with similar economic capacity—options still remain. Indeed, some older industrialized cities among the 66 examined—such as Pittsburgh and Trenton—have managed to successfully renew their economic base, and therefore increase their fiscal capacity.

This book will have made a valuable contribution if it helps to restore our awareness of the options for revitalization that lie within the grasp of government policymakers. Underlying these options are the economic fundamentals that look to the health and vigor of the private sector. *Urban Fiscal Stress* shows, quite dramatically, that municipal financial health depends above all on maintaining economic activity through private investment.

I might add that much of the rhetoric surrounding the Sunbelt/Frostbelt controversy disappears in the detailed analysis in *Urban Fiscal Stress*. Fiscal stress is not a regional phenomenon; older, industrially-aged cities—those most prone to stress—are located in all regions of the country. Moreover, even rapidly growing cities may experience fiscal stress if their financial patterns outpace their economic resources.

For someone now in my present position, directing a large public school system, the emphasis on the responsibilities and opportunities of the private sector that emerges from this book is especially encouraging. Clearly, jobs for the next generation of city residents must come largely from the private sector. A first-rate educational system can be a key ingredient in attracting business firms to the city. Recent surveys have indicated that the quality of services, such as education, can be an effective locational inducement to business. The real stumbling block is the high cost of services in older cities which contributes to fiscal stress and discourages private investment. If state governments were to assume a greater share of the cost of such services, fiscal problems would be measurably reduced, easing the way for an improved environment for private investment.

Admittedly, regardless of which level of government pays for services, we must accept some constraints on the overall growth of the public sector if the trade-off is a vigorous expansion in private job opportunities. Nonetheless, education—in a world of budgetary constraints—has a unique role to play. Of all services, education can have an especially direct pay-off in terms of economic growth by providing the trained labor force to fill emerging jobs. If we are prudent and recognize that the link between public education and private investment is an essential condition for urban revitalization, then we will have moved the debate over national urban policy onto new ground.

This book is an important beginning in such a debate.

Robert C. Wood
Superintendent, Boston Public Schools
Former Secretary,
U.S. Department of Housing and Urban Development

Preface

This study was launched in 1977 to provide new insights into municipal fiscal stress. At that time—and even more so today—there was growing concern about serious financial problems, including the potential for bankruptcy, in our cities. Virtually every individual and institution with a stake in a city has a vested interest in better understanding why municipal fiscal stress occurs and how it can be avoided.

To date, however, analysis of city financial performance has been impeded by the lack of consistent and reliable financial data. We reasoned that creating a comprehensive municipal financial data system would allow us to overcome this limitation. Therefore, we created a comprehensive financial data base from individual city annual reports and published and unpublished detailed information from the U.S. Bureau of the Census. The data were organized to assure comparability from one city to another. To analyze the way in which the external forces impact on municipal financial performance, we developed a methodological framework from well-established urban economic growth theory.

This project was undertaken jointly by the Economics Department of The First National Bank of Boston and Touche Ross & Co., which are primarily responsible for the analysis, findings, and recommendations contained in this report; nonetheless, this project could not have been completed without the advice of many others. To achieve a high degree of real-world relevancy to this project, a Municipal Advisory Board was drawn together.

The Municipal Advisory Board is composed of distinguished mayors, municipal officials, and scholars. Throughout the project the Board held periodic meetings to guide the overall direction and emphasis of the work and to participate in the selection, assessment, and interpretation of the data. The members of the Board are listed at the conclusion of this preface.

This report was prepared under the general supervision of the Council for Northeast Economic Action, a nonpartisan organization of leading public and private sector officials drawn from the nine Northeastern states. The Council was instrumental in establishing effective liaison with numerous municipal officials throughout the country, and individual Council members played an important role in the review process.

Finally, this report could not have been completed without the thoughtful research and editorial assistance of Ms. Diane Fulman, Consultant, and Ms. Barbara Eller, Assistant Vice President, The First National Bank of Boston; Mr. Irwin T. David, Partner, Mr. Ronald Brubaker, Consultant, and Ms. Diane Lansing, Director, Public Sector Program, Touche Ross & Co.

We believe that the analysis presented here has important implications for all who are concerned with municipal financial performance. Further, we believe the data base as well as the methodology in this study can help policymakers understand why fiscal stress occurs, the ways in which it can be measured, and the manner in which it can be addressed.

Four observations are required. First, we have analyzed the economic-social-structural-financial linkages for one point in time. Future analyses should examine financial performance over a longer time frame.

Second, while we have focused on fiscal stress, it may well be that fiscal stress represents the symptoms of urban problems, not the causes. Indeed, our analysis reveals that economic forces have the most notable impact on a city's fiscal condition and that older industrialized cities are most likely to be stressed because of a decline in their economic activity. This means that municipal financial well-being depends on maintaining private investment and jobs. Federal or state efforts to deal with municipal fiscal stress without addressing the investment and job creation issues may help cities with their immediate cash flow difficulties, but will not encourage them to come to terms with their underlying problems.

Third, our common treatment of expenses, taxes, and debt is effective for analysis of cities within clusters (grouped for common characteristics) and for detecting wide variances of sources and use of resources among cities across clusters. These definitions may not be equally useful for other purposes requiring detailed understanding of individual city policies and conditions related to financial management and performance.

Finally, some cities are also counties or have essentially the resources and expenses associated with the overlapping county structure. These cities are well represented (14) among the 66 cities sample. These differences—along with the variances caused by different services and service levels, and state programs and legislation—are all part of the varied city resource base and services measured in the study. Thus, the significance of the statistics is most relevant in the clusters, where a mixture of these varying conditions removes bias when examining common economic, social, and structural characteristics.

With this in mind, we are disseminating the 66 cities report in the belief that it will add to our overall understanding of municipal financial performance. We hope that the conclusions and recommendations derived from our analyses will not only encourage additional research but will also stimulate a new dialogue on national policy options to aid our cities.

Municipal Advisory Board

Part I
Overview

1

The Study: Principal Conclusions and Policy Implications

Introduction

In recent years, the fiscal condition of American cities–particularly older industrialized cities–has come under close scrutiny. This growing interest in the financial future of urban America appears to be a direct result of recent shifts in municipal finance:

> From 1960 to 1975, municipal expenditures have risen nearly 350 percent, while nominal Gross National Product rose by only 200 percent.

> Municipal debt outstanding tripled, from $23.2 billion in 1960 to $68.8 billion in 1975.

> Municipal government employment has increased by 49 percent from 1960 to 1975, from 1.7 million to 2.5 million.

> Federal aid to cities has grown from $592 million in 1960 to $10.9 billion in 1975, more than an 18-fold increase. Yet, city expenses have increased only 4.6 times. Moreover, cities throughout the country are demanding additional Federal funds.

These national developments underscore the compelling need for a more accurate and complete picture of municipal finance.

This study was launched to provide new empirical insights into the financial performance of cities with widely differing economic, social, and structural conditions. We reasoned that improving the ability to diagnose a municipality's fiscal condition would be important to policymakers at all levels of government. Mayors want to know where they stand and how much managerial "play in the line" there is in the financial structure of their particular cities. State governments, particularly those that have urban policies, want to develop means of measuring the relative fiscal strengths and weaknesses of their cities. And, there has been a renewed Federal commitment to urban fiscal issues, as is evident in the Carter Administration's national urban policy, specifically the proposed Supplementary Fiscal Assistance Act.

Yet, there is a paradox about most of the discussions of municipal fiscal stress; namely, policymakers and researchers alike proceed on the assumption that they can detect stress and determine its relative severity by reference to *socio-economic* indicators (e.g., unemployment rate, age of housing stock, etc.).

3

There appear to be two interrelated reasons why socio-economic variables are used to measure the fiscal condition of cities. First, it is assumed that socio-economic conditions cause fiscal conditions; second, it is assumed that socio-economic variables are accurate indicators of financial viability.

These assumptions seem to have a common sense foundation. After all, no city can escape the reality of its socio-economic conditions. Yet, the assumptions are certainly not a self-evident proposition. Many factors can influence the fiscal performance of cities. The level of Federal and state aid as well as state assumption of services can affect a city's financial performance. Moreover, management practices vary widely among cities, as does the municipal commitment to particular levels of service delivery. A rich man can spend himself into insolvency, while the frugal clerk succeeds in making ends meet. Might not the same be true for cities? The findings derived from the 66 Cities Study—described in the following section—provide new insight into this question.

Principal Conclusions Summarized

Our analysis revealed seven principal findings, which are briefly described below:

> *Older industrially aged cities are the ones most likely to have high tax, debt, and expense ratios and to be fiscally stressed.* Cities undergo a basic process of industrial aging. Each phase of this process is marked by changes in economic, social, and structural conditions which have a significant impact on municipal financial performance.

> *Yet some older industrialized cities do not show signs of fiscal strain, while some younger, more rapidly growing cities do.* In short, although fiscal strain generally accompanies industrial aging, this is not always the case.

> *Fiscal stress is not inevitable.* Achieving a financial equilibrium between the demand for public services and financial resources appears to be within the grasp of management control of most cities. Out of the 66 cities subjected to detailed comparative analysis, only four appear to have pushed their tax, debt, and expense rates close to or beyond sustainable limits.

> *Municipal fiscal stress cannot be described on the basis of economic, social, and structural conditions alone.* Socio-economic indicators are not valid proxies for the financial performance of cities. Measurement of a city's fiscal performance must include financial indicators.

> *Combined Federal and state grant-in-aid programs are more responsive to the social and structural problems than to the economic and financial problems of cities.* However, the results of this study show that fiscal stress appears to result more from economic problems than from social or structural problems.

Industrially mature cities are less effective in leveraging their municipal capital spending in ways to encourage private capital investment. For cities in their early growth stages, municipal capital spending levels are accompanied by increases in private manufacturing capital spending. Yet for older industrialized cities, municipal capital spending rises rapidly and then remains high, despite a fall-off in private capital spending.

Current municipal data collection and financial reporting systems are generally inadequate to understand and effectively manage city operations. Variations in municipal accounting practices produce inconsistencies and data gaps as financial performance data are analyzed across cities.

Undertaking the Analysis of Municipal Financial Performance

The interaction between social/economic/structural forces and municipal financial performance is crucial to defining and measuring municipal fiscal stress. This definition depends on the ability to isolate the impacts of these forces on municipal financial performance. A brief comment on each of these economic, social, and structural forces will be helpful in building a foundation for the subsequent analyses.

Economic conditions describe the resource base in a municipality. These conditions reflect a broad range of exogenous forces, especially manufacturing investment and private sector construction.[1] Other factors include income level and distribution, the occupational structure of the labor market, and the size and age of the resident population.

Private sector capital spending is the driving force that produces economic growth. Whenever a city is young, growing rapidly, creating substantial new jobs, and income is rising, expanding private investment will be evident. Conversely, when industrial maturity is reached, private sector capital formation will slow down. Economic conditions—especially investment—have the most significant impact on a city's financial performance inasmuch as they determine the city's level of resource capability for providing public services. Yet, economic conditions cannot be judged alone because they are influenced by social and structural conditions.

Social conditions describe the consequences of economic growth. For example, rapid private sector investment in manufacturing may induce a lower unemployment rate and the reduction of poverty among those who were previously unemployed. The condition of a municipality's housing stock, as well as the relative share of minority residents, also describes or reflects the municipality's social conditions. Yet, social conditions also include a wide range of circumstances that are distinct from economic conditions and can in themselves induce change. For example, the deterioration of the housing stock will lead to demands for increased municipal fire expenditures and increases in unemployment put pressure on the city to provide social services. Changes in social conditions can force changes in the level and mix of public services.

Structural conditions describe those factors that define the taxing and spending parameters for a city, as well as its relationship to contiguous cities and higher levels of government. These factors include the number of square miles in the city, annexation constraints, and population density. Structural factors are vitally important because the spatial dimensions of economic activity (especially investment) often overlap or fall outside of a municipality's jurisdictional boundaries. Furthermore, investment shifts from one city to another can produce dramatic changes in a municipality's tax base.

Economic, social, and structural factors, as described above, have major impacts on municipal resources and the demands on those resources. The variables reflecting these three conditions that were used in this analysis are listed as follows:

Economic Conditions (Variables)

Change in population
Percent change in single-family housing starts
Manufacturing capital spending
Change in manufacturing employment ratio
Percent change in manufacturing capital spending
Median family income

Primary source of data was the 1972 Bureau of the Census City and County Data Book. Estimates of private manufacturing capital spending were derived from the 1972 Census of Manufactures. The 1970 Census of Population was used to adjust manufacturing capital spending to per capita estimates.

Social Conditions (Variables)

Percent minority population
Percent families below low-income level
Unemployment rate
Percent pre-1939 housing stock

Estimates for pre-1939 housing stock were derived from the 1952 City and County Data Book.

Structural Conditions (Variables)

Population density[2]

The 66 cities were classified statistically into four clusters based on the six economic variables; the resulting four clusters were:

High investment and income cities

Above-average investment and income cities

Average investment and income cities

Below-average investment and income cities

Then, each of these four clusters was divided between high-low socially-dependent populations as well as between high-low structural characteristics. The resulting framework contained 16 clusters of cities that represented homogeneous economic, social, and structural conditions.

To choose the financial variables, the research team studied more than 100 financial data items. Through various statistical techniques, 13 of the 100 were selected as the basis for the study. Throughout this analysis, these 13 variables are called the Short List of Municipal Financial Performance Variables (or the Short List of Financial Variables), indicating that they provide substantive insight into the larger set of data from which they were drawn. Unless otherwise noted, all financial data used in the study are for 1975.[3]

The financial variables are listed in Table 1.1, along with the standard deviation, highest, lowest, and average values for each.

Data on these economic, social, structural, and financial variables were collected and analyzed for 66 medium-to-large cities across the country. All cities with populations over 1,000,000 were excluded from the analysis to avoid distorting the results of the study. It is generally recognized that very large cities possess economic, social, and structural conditions that make them unique, thus making comparative analyses with medium-sized cities difficult.

The 66 cities analyzed in the study are listed in Table 1.2. These cities may be briefly characterized as follows. The mean population size was approximately 250,000. The largest city analyzed was Baltimore (population 905.8 thousand) while the smallest was Rochester, Minnesota (population 53.8 thousand). The regional distribution is shown in Table 1.3.

Within each of the sixteen clusters, the mean values were calculated for the Short List of Municipal Financial Performance Variables. These data were the basis for analyzing the linkages between various sets of municipal economic, social, and structural conditions and financial performance.

The detailed analyses are described in the "Method and Analysis" Section of this report. The following section summarizes the basis for each of the conclusions.

The Principal Conclusions in Detail

Older Industrially Aged Cities Are the Ones Most Likely to Have High Tax, Debt, and Expense Ratios and to Be Fiscally Stressed. As a city passes through

Table 1.1
The Short List of Municipal Financial Performance Variables

Financial Variables	Mean Value	Standard Deviation	Lowest Value	Highest Value
Revenue:				
Ratio of local taxes to personal income (tax effort)	5.65%	2.26%	1.92%	13.42%
Local taxes per capita	$265.02	$106.41	$98.76	$556.36
Intergovernmental revenue as a percent of total local revenue	34.60%	12.24%	5.00%	64.00%
Debt:				
Total debt per capita	$516.86	$268.59	$121.66	$1,193.84
Interest per capita	$23.19	$14.30	$5.32	$89.69
Municipal capital spending per capita, five-year average, 1971-75	$81.52	$46.75	$20.55	$223.25
Expense:				
Fire expenses per capita	$29.55	$10.32	$9.48	$56.42
Education expenses per capita (total from all sources)	$236.94	$60.24	$120.45	$395.08
Health expenses per capita (total from all sources)	$7.56	$9.07	$0.00[a]	$47.11
Welfare expenses per capita (total from all sources)	$5.52	$14.81	$0.00[a]	$92.22
Ratio of city full-time-equivalent employment to total local employment	3.98%	2.23%	0.95%	10.58%
Average city employee annual income	$7,746	$1,606	$4,158	$12,319
Current operating expenses per capita	$484.61	$120.27	$270.40	$928.36

[a]A zero value for health and welfare means that the entire expenses of these programs are borne by other levels of government.

its various stages of development, there are important impacts on municipal financial performance. Private sector capital spending—especially in the manufacturing sector—follows a clear pattern. Cities in their early growth stages generally have rapid and extensive private sector investment as well as substantial population growth. As cities pass into the stage of industrial maturity, there is a fall-off in investment and, in turn, a sustained loss of manufacturing employment.

There is a strong correspondence, but not a precise fit, between the four economic clusters and the stages of industrial development. Several factors account for the differences. Those cities just beginning to generate significant levels of private investment and those experiencing declining investment may both have, for a period of time, relatively similar investment levels. Also, a city can "buck" the economic aging process to some extent through successful

Table 1.2
The 66 Cities

1. Mobile AL	34. Cambridge MA
2. Montgomery AL	35. Springfield MA
3. Phoenix AZ	36. Worcester MA
4. Tempe AZ	37. Grand Rapids MI
5. Tucson AZ	38. Bloomington MN
6. Little Rock AR	39. Duluth MN
7. Daly City CA	40. Minneapolis MN
8. Fresno CA	41. Rochester MN
9. Long Beach CA	42. Jackson MS
10. Pasadena CA	43. Kansas City MO
11. Denver CO	44. Lincoln NB
12. Pueblo CO	45. Omaha NB
13. Bridgeport CT	46. Trenton NJ
14. Hartford CT	47. Albuquerque NM
15. New Haven CT	48. Buffalo NY
16. Stamford CT	49. Syracuse NY
17. Hollywood FL	50. Greensboro NC
18. Jacksonville FL	51. Dayton OH
19. St. Petersburg FL	52. Eugene OR
20. Tampa FL	53. Pittsburgh PA
21. West Palm Beach FL	54. Amarillo TX
22. Atlanta GA	55. Austin TX
23. Savannah GA	56. Fort Worth TX
24. Decatur IL	57. Galveston TX
25. Evanston IL	58. Irving TX
26. Indianapolis IN	59. Port Arthur TX
27. Topeka KS	60. San Angelo TX
28. Wichita KS	61. Salt Lake City UT
29. Louisville KY	62. Richmond VA
30. Baton Rouge LA	63. Seattle WA
31. New Orleans LA	64. Spokane WA
32. Baltimore MD	65. Madison WI
33. Boston MA	66. Milwaukee WI

renewal strategies. In such a case, the city would have been placed in a more favorable investment and income cluster than its stage of growth would warrant. Conversely, an industrially young city may have adopted policies which discourage private sector investment, thus placing it in a lower investment cluster.

The concept of industrial aging was integrated into the methodology of the study by grouping the cities according to two key factors in the aging process—population decline and manufacturing employment decline.

Old Industrialized—Cities in which manufacturing employment has declined in two consecutive periods—1954-67 and 1967-72—in which the rate of decline in manufacturing employment accelerated in the second period, and population declined in two periods—1950-60 and 1960-70. The following nine cities were classified in this category:

Bridgeport	Baltimore	Worcester
Hartford	Boston	Trenton
New Haven	Cambridge	Buffalo

Industrially Maturing—Cities in which manufacturing employment declined in the first and second periods or the second alone; population declined in the period 1960-1970. There was no acceleration in the rate of decline in manufacturing employment. The following 13 cities were determined to be in this category:

Dayton	Mobile
Pittsburgh	Pasadena
Seattle	Louisville
Spokane	New Orleans
Milwaukee	Springfield
Minneapolis	Duluth
Syracuse	

Young Industrial Growth—Cities in which both manufacturing employment and population were expanding in both of the periods analyzed (44 cities).

Our analyses of the impact of industrial aging on municipal financial performance indicate that as cities age industrially:

Taxes rise.

Current operating expenses rise.

The municipal work force increases rapidly.

These conclusions are evident from the municipal financial data shown in Table 1.4. Note specifically the increases in tax effort (the ratio of taxes to personal income), taxes per capita, and current operating expenses from young to old

Table 1.3
Regional Distribution

Region	Number of Cities in Sample
Northeast	12
Midwest	11
South	18
High Plains	5
Southwest	8
West	12
Total	66

Table 1.4

Industrial Aging and Municipal Financial Performance

Stages of Industrialization	Ratio of Local Taxes to Personal Income	Local Taxes per Capita	Current Operating Expenses per Capita	Intergov- ernmental Revenue as a Percent of Total Local Revenue	Ratio of City Full- Time-Equiv- alent Employ- ment to Total Local Employment	Ratio of Current Operating Expenses per Capita to Local Taxes per Capita
Old industrialized (9 cities)	9.50%	$407.33	$603.86	37.99%	8.01%	1.482
Industrially maturing (13 cities)	5.51	254.44	517.73	40.66	4.25	2.035
Young, early phases of industrial growth (44 cities)	4.90	239.20	450.50	32.10	3.07	1.883
Total sample mean (66 cities)	5.65%	$265.02	$484.61	34.60%	3.98%	1.829

industrialized cities. The decline in the ratio of expenses to taxes is the result of the much faster rise in taxes vis-à-vis expenses: as cities age, the percent of their total revenue from state and Federal sources tends to stabilize. As a result, local taxes must increase at a faster rate to cover rising costs. Finally, the sharp rise in the municipal work force is obvious—in the case of old industrialized cities it is more than twice as high as in the young cities.

Cities in the advanced stages of industrial aging are concentrated in the Northeastern states. The explanation for this finding is straightforward: the Industrial Revolution started first in the Northeast. Counter-intuitive is that high debt ratios are not limited to Northeastern cities; some Southern cities also have high debt rates.[4]

Table 1.5 shows that cities with high cost and tax rates are more prevalent in the Northeast, followed by the Midwest and West. This reflects the geographic distribution of the cities that are economically the oldest. The tabulation also shows the high level of debt financing by cities in the South and Northeast.

Interpretation of the regional distribution for taxes, debt, and expenses shown in Table 1.5 requires a brief explanation. Eight percent of the cities in the sample, without respect to regional location, have tax ratios that are 85 percent or more of the highest tax ratio for the 66 cities. Yet, among Northeastern cities, 42 percent of them fall into the 85 percent or more category, while none does for the remaining five regions. Note the higher average debt ratios for the Northeast and Southern cities. Moreover, the frequency distribution for Northeastern cities in terms of their current operating ratios stands in sharp contrast to the ratios of cities in other regions.

Table 1.5
Regional Frequency Distributions for Tax, Debt, and Expenses Expressed as a Percent of Maximum Value for 66 Cities[a]

Percentage Distribution	Total Sample	North-east	Mid-west	South	High Plains	South-west	West
For local taxes per capita:							
Less than 25%	11%	–	9%	12%	40%	18%	–
26-50%	52	25%	36	71	40	82	40%
51-75%	27	33	45	18	20	–	50
76-85%	3	–	9	–	–	–	10
More than 85%	8	42	–	–	–	–	–
For total debt per capita:							
Less than 25%	20%	8%	18%	18%	–	27%	40%
26-50%	55	50	55	59	60%	55	50
51-75%	12	17	18	6	40	9	–
76-85%	3	8	–	–	–	9	–
More than 85%	11	17	9	18	–	–	10
For current operating expenses per capita:							
Less than 25%	–	–	–	–	–	–	–
26-50%	42%	8%	18%	47%	80%	82%	40%
51-75%	52	83	82	53	20	18	60
76-85%	5	–	–	–	–	–	–
More than 85%	2	8	–	–	–	–	–

[a]Totals may not add to 100% due to rounding.

Yet Some Older Industrialized Cities Do Not Show Signs of Fiscal Strain while Some Younger, More Rapidly Growing Cities Do. Some old industrialized cities have "bucked the trend" of high per capita taxes, debt, and expenditures that are strongly associated with industrial aging. Conversely, young cities do not necessarily avoid high per capita taxes, debt, and expenditures. Several young cities studied have financial patterns that are typical of old industrialized cities. These appear to be "younger variants" of their older counterparts.

Table 1.6 illustrates the fiscal situation for two cities of each type drawn from the data base. There are other cities that may be classified in either of these two categories, but the financial data for these four illustrate this finding. Pittsburgh and Trenton can be characterized as "trend buckers," while Atlanta and Denver are "younger variants." (The means for each city's economic cluster are also shown in parentheses below the financial performance variables.)

Note that, although Pittsburgh and Trenton are industrially maturing and old industrialized cities, their tax, debt, and expenses have been managed or controlled and are either below the total sample mean or are very close to it. Moreover, their tax, debt, and operating expense rates are consistently below the means for their economic clusters. This is especially significant because method-ologically the clusters group cities with similar underlying economic capacity.[5]

Table 1.6
"Trend Buckers and Younger Variants" among the 66 Cities

Financial Variable	City				For Total 66 Cities Sample	
	"Trend Buckers"		"Younger Variants"		Sample Mean	Sample Standard Deviation
	Pittsburgh	Trenton	Atlanta	Denver		
Local taxes per capita	$227.07 (327.95)	$333.64 (360.00)	$334.19 (218.73)	$442.14 (283.44)	$265.02	$106.41
Total debt per capita	502.79 (515.95)	283.07 (661.59)	1,072.52 (504.01)	595.13 (430.78)	516.86	268.59
Current operating expenses per capita	438.86 (551.66)	530.31 (618.21)	659.94 (469.79)	615.16 (483.72)	484.61	120.27

That Trenton and Pittsburgh are well below their respective means certainly suggests that—relative to other cities with roughly comparable economic resources—their municipal financial performance has been well controlled. Conversely, the figures for Denver and Atlanta are well above the means of their economic cluster, showing that their financial commitments have exceeded those of cities with similar economic capacity.

Thus, contrary to much contemporary thinking, cities can maintain a fundamental equilibrium between economic resources and financial performance—as have Pittsburgh and Trenton—even as they reach the advanced stage of industrial aging. On the other hand, Atlanta and Denver offer insight into industrially younger cities whose financial spending has grown more rapidly than their economic base, thus pushing their tax, debt, and expense ratios more in line with those of older cities. Note especially Denver's high tax ratio, Atlanta's high debt ratio, and the high operating expenses for both cities.

Fiscal Stress Is Not Inevitable. As the preceding conclusions indicate, there are some cities that do not fit the expected patterns. Some mature cities have low tax, debt, and expense ratios while some younger ones have high ratios. The analysis suggests that the management and political decision-making processes can hold the growth of services in balance with underlying economic resources to maintain financial equilibrium, even under adverse economic, social, and structural conditions. Moreover, no city with high expense rates *per se* should be considered stressed, if it has the underlying economic capacity to fund high rates of spending. In other words, the concept of fiscal stress must take into account the underlying resources—the capacity to support tax, debt, or spending.

The cities in each of the 16 clusters are confronted with very similar external forces. Thus, it was possible to identify cities whose financial response deviated from that of cities with comparable economic capacities. On the other hand, lower-than-expected municipal financial performance could indicate un-derutilized resource capacity.[6]

To develop a more complete understanding of the linkage between resource capacity and spending rates as well as to refine the concept of stress, all cities which had tax, debt, or expense rates greater than one standard deviation from the cluster means were analyzed further. These are shown in Table 1.7.

A number of generalizations may be made about the cities classified as outliers in Table 1.7:

Only 4 cities out of the 66—Stamford, Boston, Hartford, and Atlanta—fall outside one standard deviation in terms of their tax, debt, and expense ratios within their economic clusters. Eight additional cities—Denver, Bloomington, Seattle, Worcester, Duluth, Long Beach, Richmond, and Fresno—are outside one standard deviation in two of the three key financial performance measures. Relative to other cities in their clusters, the tax, debt, and expense rates of these cities are high, which suggests that they are near or beyond their underlying resource capacity.

The 12 cities are scattered throughout the extreme variations in good and bad economic, social, and structural clusters. For the 3 old industrialized cities—Hartford, Boston, and Worcester—this may well imply fiscal stress. Two industrially maturing cities, Duluth and Seattle, are also out of line with their economically grouped city counterparts. The remaining 7 cities were classified as young growth in terms of their age of industrialization and provide additional insight into the issue of "younger variants." Yet these high expenses, taxes, and debt may not necessarily be a sign of imminent stress in these cities because of their stronger economic base.

Importantly, 54 cities—the vast majority—appear to have maintained their tax, debt, and expense ratios in line with underlying resource capacity. At the least, it may be argued that their tax, debt, and expense rates are relatively close to the individual cluster means. This indicates a generally consistent response to the homogeneous/exogenous economic, social, and structural forces.

Finally, the regional mix of the stressed cities is shown in Table 1.8. The high incidence of Northeastern cities was expected. The Western and Southern cities may well be the "younger variants" of their Northeastern counterparts. As stated in an earlier finding, this suggests that these cities may respond in a financial manner characteristic of industrially mature cities, although they have not yet reached that stage of economic development.

Municipal Fiscal Stress Cannot Be Described on the Basis of Economic, Social, and Structural Conditions Alone. Social, economic, and structural variables have often been used to indicate the fiscal condition of cities. In contrast, this study shows socio-economic conditions are not necessarily valid proxies for the

Table 1.7

Fiscal Stress: Cities with Taxing, Debt, and Spending Rates Greater than One Standard Deviation from the Means of Their Economic Clusters

Cluster	Number of Cities in Cluster	Cities with Tax Performance Greater than One Standard Deviation above Cluster Mean	Cities with Debt Performance Greater than One Standard Deviation above Cluster Mean	Cities with Expense Performance Greater than One Standard Deviation above Cluster Mean
High private investment and income:				
Large dependent population	2	(Insufficient data in cluster)		
Small dependent population	7	Denver	Bloomington	Denver
			Baton Rouge	
High population density	3	(Insufficient data in cluster)		
Low population density	6	Bloomington	Baton Rouge	Bloomington
Above-average private investment and income:				
Large dependent population	6	Evanston	Kansas City	
Small dependent population	6	Stamford	Stamford	Stamford
High population density	6	Evanston	Seattle	Seattle
Low population density	6	Stamford	Stamford	Stamford
Average private investment and income:				
Large dependent population	13	Boston	Louisville	Pasadena
			Boston	Dayton
				Boston
Small dependent population	13	Cambridge	Eugene	Duluth
		Worcester	Wichita	Worcester
				Minneapolis
High population density	11	Cambridge	Louisville	Pasadena
		Boston	Minneapolis	Dayton
			Boston	Boston
Low population density	15	Worcester	Eugene	Duluth
			Duluth	Worcester
			Wichita	
Below-average private investment and income:				
Large dependent population	14	New Haven	Hartford	Hartford
		Hartford	Richmond	
		Richmond	Atlanta	
Small dependent population	5	Long Beach		Long Beach
High population density	5	Hartford	Hartford	Hartford
Low population density	14	Fresno	Richmond	Fresno
		Richmond	Atlanta	Tampa
		Atlanta		Atlanta

financial performance of cities. To describe fiscal condition indirectly, solely on the basis of social, economic, and structural variables, could result in classifying some cities as financially stressed when, in fact, they are not.

To demonstrate this, Table 1.9 shows six cities that are classified as fiscally

Table 1.8
Regional Mix of Fiscally Stressed Cities

Region	Number of Cities with 2 or 3 Ratios in Excess of One Standard Deviation	Total Sample
Northeast	4	12
South	2	18
Southwest	—	8
Midwest	2	11
High Plains	—	5
West	4	12
Total	12	66

stressed or troubled in six widely used studies that purport to statistically measure municipal stress, along with their comparative rankings. The lower the ranking, the greater the degree of fiscal stress.

The 66 cities in our study are not classified in terms of best-to-worst

Table 1.9
Comparative Ranking of Cities (According to Recent Studies)

City	U.S. Treasury[a]	Brookings Institution Urban Conditions[b]	Brookings Institution Hardship Index[c]	Clark Study[d]	National Planning Association Study[e]	Urban Institute Study[f]
Buffalo	3	3	9	5	9	14
Fort Worth	17	NA	19	20	37	NA
Indianapolis	24	NA	23	NA	14	NA
Pittsburgh	26	6	15	16	8	13
Baltimore	32	9	6	NA	5	18
Jacksonville	43	NA	NA	8	20	NA
Total cities analyzed	48	489	550	54	40	153

NA = Not analyzed in this investigation.

[a]U.S. Department of Treasury, "Report on the Fiscal Impact of the Economic Stimulus Package on Forty-Eight Large Governments," January 23, 1978, Washington, D.C.

[b]Richard Nathan, "Decentralizing Community Development," Report to the Department of Housing and Urban Development, January 1978, Brookings Institution, Washington, D.C.

[c]Richard Nathan, Charles Adams, "Understanding Central City Hardship," *Political Science Quarterly*, Volume 91, Number 1, Spring 1976, pp. 47-62, Washington, D.C.

[d]Terry Clark, et al., "How Many New Yorks—New York Fiscal Crisis in Comparative Perspective," University of Chicago, July 5, 1976, Chicago.

[e]John Craig and Michael Kolleda, "Outlook for the Municipal Hospital in Major American Cities," National Planning Association, April 1976, Washington, D.C.

[f]Harvey A. Garn, Thomas Muller, et al., "A Framework for National Urban Policy," The Urban Institute, December 15, 1977, Washington, D.C.

financial performance. It was felt that comparative municipal financial performance should be undertaken with reference to a number of financial performance indicators rather than a single index number. The 13 variables in the Short List of Municipal Financial Performance Variables capture a large amount of financial variance across cities. Additional statistical refinement can be achieved by adding other variables in specific areas.

The relevant financial data from this study for these six cities are shown in Table 1.10. Comparison of the various rankings of these six cities shows widely different results; when ranked according to various socio-economic criteria, some cities are classified as stressed. Yet these same cities ranked according to financial criteria alone may not show fiscal stress.

Note that the tax per capita ratio for five of these cities is below the average of the total sample, and the tax ratio for the remaining city lies well inside one standard deviation from the sample mean.

Clearly, there is greater variance in the debt ratios as only three cities fall below the sample mean. But again, note that all of the remaining debt ratios are roughly equal to or below one standard deviation.

Four of the six cities have total operating ratios roughly equal to or below the sample mean, and the remaining two cities fall well within one standard deviation.

Although not shown in Table 1.10, it is important to also point out that the tax, debt, and operating expense rates for these six cities are well within one standard deviation of the means for each of their respective economic clusters. This is especially relevant because the economic clusters have been designed to capture homogeneous exogenous forces that impact on the cities.

Table 1.10
Key Financial Performance Data for Cities Classified as "Fiscally Stressed" on the Basis of Socio-Economic Variables

City	Local Taxes per Capita	Total Debt per Capita	Current Operating Expenses per Capita
Buffalo	$234.27	$707.56	$595.22
Fort Worth	204.81	474.75	382.87
Indianapolis	197.92	396.99	348.97
Pittsburgh	227.07	502.79	438.86
Baltimore	312.65	553.50	514.18
Jacksonville	164.90	554.41	489.61
Total 66 cities mean	$265.02	$516.86	$484.61
Total standard deviation	$106.41	$268.59	$120.27

The financial performance measures for Fort Worth, Indianapolis, Pittsburgh, and Jacksonville do not indicate that these cities are "fiscally stressed" when compared to the average performance of the 66 cities. Buffalo and Baltimore present a less clear and convincing picture. Buffalo may have higher-than-average debt and operating expense ratios, but certainly not higher tax rates. This may, in part, be explained by Buffalo's very high rate of intergovernmental transfers. Expenses are high in Baltimore, but this by no means leads one to conclude that Baltimore is fiscally stressed.

This does not mean that socio-economic factors are unimportant. To the contrary, the indicators used in these studies are excellent measures of socio-economic problems which unquestionably affect a city's financial performance. However, the focus of new research is shifting to include municipal fiscal conditions. Therefore, to measure fiscal conditions, financial measures are needed.

Combined Federal and State Grant-in-Aid Programs Are More Responsive to the Social and Structural Problems than to the Economic and Financial Problems of Cities. While the Federal and state grant-in-aid system is responsive to social and structural needs, it frequently fails to target funds to cities with the greatest economic and financial problems. Generally, large intergovernmental transfer payments go to ,those cities with adverse social and structural conditions. In contrast, the percent of transfer payments may, under some conditions, be less to cities with below-average investment vis-à-vis those with high investment. These points emerged from the analysis of patterns in intergovernmental aid across the four principal economic clusters as social conditions shift from small-to-large dependent population ratios and as population densities shift from low to high. This shows what happened to intergovernmental aid under different economic, social, and structural conditions.

In principle, intergovernmental transfers[7] are designed to reduce income disparities and alleviate social problems across cities with widely differing conditions (equalization). Historically, these transfers have been largely targeted to improve educational, housing, health, welfare, and other social functions. Among the more than 500 Federal grant-in-aid programs, few are directed specifically at stimulating economic growth. Thus, while there has been an increasing need for fiscal and economic assistance, this has not yet been reflected in the transfer allocations. The relevant data for intergovernmental revenue are contained in Table 1.11.

The statistical swing data[8] in Table 1.11 show the sensitivity of these income transfers, as economic conditions change across the clusters (social and structural conditions held constant) or as social and structural conditions change (economic conditions held constant). As economic conditions worsen among large social dependent population and high population density cities, the percent of intergovernmental transfer income actually declines somewhat, in contrast to

Table 1.11
Intergovernmental Revenue as a Percent of Total Local Revenue

Social/Structural Conditions	High Investment and Income Cluster Cities	Below-Average Investment and Income Cluster Cities	Percent Swing Between Economic Clusters
Small social dependent population	30.2%	33.3%	+10.3%
Large social dependent population	43.0	37.5	−12.8
Low population density	30.4	35.9	+18.1
High population density	38.3	37.6	−1.8
Percent swing as social/density conditions worsen:			
Small to large social dependent population	+42.4%	+12.6%	
Low to high population density	+26.0	+4.7	

what may be expected. At the same time, among the low-service-dependent population and low-population-density cities these transfers increase somewhat as economic conditions deteriorate. The swings in the large social-dependent and high-population-density cities as economic conditions deteriorate are counter-intuitive.

Furthermore, the biggest differences in transfer payments are associated with unfavorable social and structural problems rather than adverse economic conditions. Note that the best economic cities with a large social-dependent population get more Federal and state funds than cities with poor economies but a relatively small social-dependent population. The economically well-off cities with large social problems receive the highest percentage of transfers for the sample. This suggests that cities qualify incrementally for more Federal and state funds as social problems become more pronounced, irrespective of their economic conditions.

On the basis of this analysis, the intergovernmental transfer system seems to be somewhat more responsive to unfavorable social and structural conditions than to adverse economic conditions. Increasingly, however, national attention is being focused on municipal fiscal stability. Therefore, Federal and state officials should be aware that past funding patterns may not alleviate severe fiscal difficulties in cities with a large service-dependent population that experience an economic downturn.

Specifically, the economically troubled city is pressed simultaneously on two fronts: no increase in intergovernmental transfers and, as was described in the first conclusion, a rapid rise in expenses. As intergovernmental fund percentages level off, taxes are driven upward.

Additional support for this finding is the performance of intergovernmental transfers across the 26 cities in the average investment and income economic cluster. This cluster is especially interesting because it includes cities in the old industrialized stage of development (5 cities), cities in the industrially maturing stage (9 cities), and cities in the young, early phases of their industrialization (12 cities). Aside from Baltimore, the remainder of the old industrialized cities in this cluster are receiving a smaller percentage of transfer payments than the industrially maturing cities.

This finding needs additional investigation—specifically on a program-by-program basis—but it is clear that while industrial aging and higher taxes and expenses go together, intergovernmental transfers and industrial aging may not. This relationship is interesting inasmuch as there is a strong need among the old industrialized cities both to keep taxes within manageable levels and to encourage private sector investment.

Industrially Mature Cities Are Less Effective in Leveraging Their Municipal Capital Spending in Ways to Encourage Private Capital Investment. The first two conclusions addressed the impact of industrial aging on municipal financial performance. There are also special effects on municipal capital spending for infrastructure and private investment. As cities age industrially, they are less likely to leverage their municipal capital spending in ways to encourage private capital investment. Moreover, the slowdown in the growth of the city's economic base occurs at the same time as the demand for services rises—just when the city can least afford to have its resources stagnate or decline.

The relevant ratios shown in Table 1.12 tell an important story about industrial aging and municipal financial performance. Reading the data from the

Table 1.12
Industrial Aging and Municipal/Private Capital Spending

Economic Cluster	Stage of Industrialization	Total Debt per Capita	Municipal Capital Spending per Capita, Five-Year Average, 1971-75	Private Manufac- turing Capital Spending per Capita, 1972	Ratio of Municipal Capital Spending to Munici- pal Debt	Ratio of Private to Municipal Capital Spending
Below-average investment/income	Old industrialized	$738.03	$133.39	$ 77.54	.180	.581
Average invest- ment/income	Old industrialized	523.08	143.75	111.88	.275	.778
Average invest- ment/income	Industrially maturing	527.84	91.07	112.08	.172	1.231
Average invest- ment/income	Young industrial growth	437.23	58.67	117.69	.134	2.001
Below-average investment/income	Young industrial growth	514.51	73.94	96.04	.144	1.299
Mean of 66 cities	–	$516.86	$ 81.52	$106.64	.158	1.308

bottom, the age of industrialization shifts from the youngest to the oldest. The higher the number in the last column, the greater the leveraging ratio, and presumably the better off is the city. The municipal debt ratio is included because of its relationship to municipal capital spending.

Two important conclusions are supported by the figures in Table 1.12:

Municipal debt and capital spending rise, albeit irregularly, as industrial aging takes place. Older cities have higher ratios of capital spending-to-debt than younger cities.

Private sector manufacturing spending peaks in the young stage of industrial aging and then falls off abruptly. This means that younger, faster growth cities "leverage" their municipal capital spending in ways to encourage private capital investment. This flattening in manufacturing capital spending is the result of—and may also contribute to—the disappearance of a cost-effective investment environment in the city vis-à-vis alternative suburban and other regional sites.

Current Municipal Data Collection and Financial Reporting Systems Are Generally Inadequate to Understand and Effectively Manage City Operations. The pervasiveness of the municipal data problem is shown by the fact that half the cities originally intended to be studied had to be excluded altogether because too much data were missing. Originally, 120 cities were to be studied. For the cities that were included a generally reliable data base was established. Yet even for these cities, there were problems. A major problem was inconsistency of data: for example, expenses are defined in widely differing ways from one city to another. Other problems included insufficient detail and, once again, lack of the desired information. Specific problems included:

Lack of information on pension fund liabilities.

Lack of breakdown by source for taxes. Therefore, for example, the residential versus corporate tax burden could not be evaluated.

Difficulty in matching capital expenditure items with their revenue source and, conversely, matching long-term debt with the proper expenditure item. Hence, it was virtually impossible to determine what portions of capital expenditures were being financed by current revenue, or to evaluate the uses of debt.

Inability to determine uses of short-term debt, i.e., tax anticipation notes versus bond anticipation notes.

Inability to determine market value of taxable property. These figures, even when available, are typically understated because industrial property changes hands infrequently.

Lack of information on the condition of long-term assets.

Some of this information could have been gathered from extensive interviews with city officials. However, this kind of effort was beyond the scope of this project. Importantly, it is also beyond the effort that could be expected by investors or officials of other levels of government.

Implications

What do these conclusions mean? How can they be used by policymakers and researchers? We believe that this study is relevant both to all levels of government and to the private sector.

At the Federal Level

These conclusions suggest that if Federal policymakers want to aid cities that are now financially troubled and to help prevent fiscal stress in the future, changes in funding patterns and allocation criteria may be most productive.

Federal Aid Designed to Combat Fiscal Stress Should Be Distributed on the Basis of Criteria Weighted Strongly Toward Municipal Financial Condition. The study shows clearly that nonfinancial variables do not accurately describe the financial condition of a city. Using financial criteria in the funding formulas is needed to assure that aid to relieve fiscal stress reaches cities that are, in fact, stressed. This is not to suggest that all Federal programs should rely on financial funding criteria. Programs to remedy social problems should logically use social indicators in the grant distribution formula or requirements. However, aid to relieve fiscal stress will better reach the cities intended to be served by the program if financial criteria are used instead of nonfinancial criteria.

Federal Aid Designed to Prevent Fiscal Stress and to Promote Financial Stability in the Long Term Should Be Most Effective If It Is Targeted at Strengthening the Economic Base of Cities, Notably by Encouraging Private Investment and Private Sector Job Creation. The study shows that deteriorating economic conditions create the greatest financial pressures on cities. While social and structural problems are important in this respect, they have less impact on a city's financial well-being than do economic problems. Therefore, fiscal stress may be best averted by programs designed to stabilize or enhance economic conditions. Of course, economic stimulus should not be the only objective of Federal aid, to the exclusion of social and other goals. However, to the extent that Federal policymakers emphasize economic and fiscal problems, careful consideration will have to be given to the trade-offs between meeting current needs and meeting long-range economic needs.

Programs Designed to Remedy Financial and Economic Problems Must Be Accurately Targeted and Appropriately Controlled to Assure that the Intent of Each Program Is Fulfilled. The study shows clearly the importance of sound planning and management in avoiding fiscal stress. Such planning and management quality should be encouraged through the design of economic and financial assistance programs. Moreover, targeting of funds to specified purposes, use of performance requirements, development of management incentives, and even the formulation of new types of grant programs that combine such targeting, management requirements, and incentives with local discretionary authority are the types of tools that can assure productive use of Federal aid.

At the State Level

State aid to cities now accounts for approximately one-third of city revenues. Therefore, all the implications described above for Federal policymakers apply as well to state officials. At the same time, states have a unique role to play in assisting cities.

There is an emerging interest in developing new ways to monitor municipal fiscal conditions. The states can be central in this regard. The Advisory Council for Intergovernmental Relations completed a study in 1973 entitled "City Financial Emergencies: The Intergovernmental Dimension" which dealt largely with the state role in helping cities avoid and overcome municipal fiscal stress. In this study, the ACIR recommends that "each state designate or establish a single state agency responsible for the improvement of local management functions such as accounting, auditing, and reporting. The Commission further recommends that the agencies be responsible for early detection of financial problems in order to prevent local financial crises."

An Early Warning System on Fiscal Stress Could Be Developed Based on the Short List of Financial Variables Used in This Study. Such a system would permit detection of fiscal stress while there is still adequate time for constructive resolution of the underlying problems. The Federal government could refine the details of such a program and encourage the states to implement the system as part of national urban policy. Alternatively, states might compete for special grant funds to develop such a system on a pilot basis (using, for example, Section 701 funds from the Department of Housing and Urban Development or Section 302 funds from the Economic Development Administration).

At the Municipal Level

The analysis reveals that, while Federal and state aid is important, revenues from local sources remain the backbone of most cities' capacity to deliver public services. The data further suggest that there is considerable latitude for changing or increasing operations within the resource limits of most cities. Most operate well below the level of tax and debt ratios that are carried by some of the oldest cities. Thus, many cities can absorb the demands of aging now—their concern is for the future. Yet even some industrially mature cities show that financial equilibrium can be achieved late in the aging process, although this has often happened only through difficult program and employment reductions needed to combat severe fiscal problems.

The point is that the success of these older cities, along with the widely differing patterns of fiscal performance by cities with similar economic, social, and structural conditions, highlight the importance of management and political decision-making in avoiding fiscal stress. Following are key implications for municipal policy makers.

City Officials Must Improve Municipal Budgeting and Planning. City officials should regularly address such key issues as: Where is the city today in terms of its resource base and the segments that require public services? Is the city growing? Maturing? What are the city's objectives? How is the city changing? What public investments and programs will best provide needed services and encourage economic growth or stability?

As has already been indicated, current accounting and reporting practices in cities are inadequate to answer many of these questions. The data base clearly needs to be improved. In addition, capital planning should be integrated into the city's central budgeting and financial management system in those cities where operating and capital budgeting are now separate, unrelated processes.

Another important problem is one of timing: elected and appointed officials are pressed to produce results within a single term of office. Yet major investment projects that could encourage development of the city's economic base require more time. In addition, cities faced with taxpayer revolts may find it increasingly difficult to fund expensive capital projects. Funding, in this instance, is a matter of prioritization which can only be determined by elected officials and the citizenry.

Cities Must Leverage Municipal Capital Spending in Ways that Develop Their Economic Resource Base. Maintaining the economic base through private investment is critical to maintaining revenue from local sources. In younger cities, this investment occurs relatively spontaneously. However, maturing and older cities must allocate both capital and services toward maintaining this process. In some cases this may require difficult trade-offs between immediate social services versus long-term job opportunities and tax base growth. But the private/public investment partnership is essential in dealing with potential fiscal stress.

Importantly, all public resources should be used to their most efficient advantage, including Federal and state aid. Often in the past, such aid has been directed at and used to expand programs or displace normal operating costs. As a result, these funds have been more a contributor to, than a solution for, fiscal problems. As economic conditions deteriorate, these funds may not grow proportionally. If Federal or state allocations change, the city is left to fund particular services on its own. More attention must be given to directing these funds to strengthening the economic base.

Cities Must Strive to Improve Their Structural Conditions to Strengthen Their Economic Bases. Structural factors affecting the cities' costs and revenues are significantly associated with stress. Those cities able to alter their boundaries or revenue base through annexation or other measures were able to prolong the periods of fiscal stability and to moderate increases in debt and taxes. Though these changes do not alter the industrial aging process, they are important in an overall program to manage' fiscal stress. Where legal or regulatory barriers to structural reform exist, they should be reviewed for their impact on all jurisdictions and modified as appropriate.

Public Officials Must Adjust Operations and Spending to Match Stabilizing or Declining Resource Bases as Their Cities Age Industrially. Many cities are already taking advantage of opportunities to improve service delivery by streamlining operations instead of increasing costs. However, even such improvements can be made only up to a certain point. After that, many cities face painful budget decisions.

The conclusions suggest that there is more opportunity than is generally realized for cities to operate within their financial resources. Prioritizing city needs can help to adjust spending to a limited, even declining, resource base while city officials simultaneously attempt to rebuild the economic base. Trenton and Pittsburgh have done just this.

Public and Private Sectors

Two key recommendations can effectively be carried out by either government agencies, quasi-public bodies, private institutions, or a combination of these entities:

Uniform Municipal Financial Accounting and Reporting Standards Should Be Developed and Adopted. The first step is to determine which body or organization is to be responsible for developing and updating accounting and reporting standards for local government. Currently, several organizations are working on various aspects of this problem, but no single entity has yet addressed the entire issue. We would anticipate a strong and continuing role for the Municipal Finance Officers Association and the National Council on Governmental Accounting, as well as others, in conjunction with the American Institute of Certified Public Accountants and the Financial Accounting Standards Board to resolve these issues.

Once the standards are defined, the next step is to ensure their uniform adoption. Upgrading municipal accounting and reporting systems will surely be time-consuming and costly at the outset. However, the potential benefits from such uniform practices present a compelling case for adopting improved standards. These benefits include improved management, increased investor confidence, more accurate bond ratings, and more equitable distribution of state and Federal aid. While it could be argued that the first three should be left to the prerogative of each city, the last benefit, distribution of intergovernmental aid, cannot. Since state and Federal aid now accounts for nearly half of most municipal budgets, it is in the interest of all concerned that the information on which this aid is based accurately reflect the condition of the cities to which it is directed.

Certainly, voluntary adoption of new accounting and reporting standards is to be hoped for. However, the track record of cities in adopting even existing standards on accounting, reporting, and disclosure has not been encouraging. The importance of the matter is such that, should voluntary adoption not succeed, legislation or regulation may be required to achieve nationwide conformance.

Additional Research Should Be Undertaken, Targeted to Improving Municipal Financial Management. In the course of this project, several key additional research topics became apparent that could potentially identify important cause and effect relationships that determine municipal financial patterns. Further study in these areas could produce information that could enhance municipal economic growth or stability in the face of industrial aging.

Examination of public capital spending and private investment to determine more precisely the cause and effect linkages between the two. This linkage refers, specifically, to the role of municipal "leveraging" in encouraging private investment. Such findings could be of great use in assisting cities to strengthen their capital spending to stabilize or enhance their economic base, thus providing a new dimension to the local "boot strapping" of the city economy.

Analysis of the behavior of municipal finances over longer time periods, including business cycle peaks and troughs to identify how city financial performance is affected by cyclical changes or by longer-run structural shifts. Real economic activity will most certainly have at least some impact on the financial well-being of municipalities whose local economic bases are vulnerable to these swings. Conversely, some municipalities are well protected from business cycle changes, either through judicious management or the fortuitous historical evolution of the industrial mix in the community. Yet despite claims to the contrary, little is actually known about this phenomenon. Further research could perhaps identify whether and how municipal management can successfully offset some of the adverse consequences of the business cycle.

Examination of the relationship of a city's stage of industrial aging to changes in taxes. The study disclosed that, while expenditures rise as a city matures industrially, taxes rise at a relatively faster rate. To the extent that high taxes hasten stagnation and the exodus of industry from older industrialized cities, this finding is significant and merits more research.

Application of the 66 cities study methodology and approach to data collection and analysis to small cities. Ultimately, improved accounting and reporting standards will greatly facilitate analysis of cities of all sizes. In the interim, it would be extremely useful to provide a data base on small cities which often have very difficult problems that differ from those of larger municipalities. Such a data base would support improved planning and better allocation of intergovernmental aid. Funding for such a project could be provided under Section 113 of the Housing and Community Development Act of the Department of Housing and Urban Development.

Notes

1. Exogenous forces, such as the cyclical swings in the national economy, will generally be reflected in shifts in industry location, investment expansion and decline, and national and state economic policies.

2. This variable could possibly have been used to provide insight into social conditions in a municipality. However, we chose it as a variable to differentiate cities along structural lines. We were specifically interested in a variable that would reflect variations in the tax base, thus providing insight into the extent to which annexation policies have or have not altered the size of the local economic base.

3. The data were adjusted to make comparison among cities statistically valid; also the data were normalized to account for population and economic differences.

4. High debt may, of course, represent a heavy reliance on industrial bond financing, or high rates of infrastructure development.

5. Trenton's above-average ratio of Federal and state aid may help to keep local taxes and debt down. However, since many Federal/state programs require matching funds, more aid can induce additional local expenses rather than save

local revenues. Nonetheless, cities with good grants management programs logically ought to fare better than cities which lack this management capability.

6. Unquestionably, factors other than capacity—i.e., local preferences—may influence municipal financial performance. These factors cannot, however, be quantified for purposes of statistical analysis. To assess the willingness of local citizens to support high taxes, expenses, and debt—as contrasted with what they are economically capable of supporting—one must examine local political and attitudinal factors.

7. Intergovernmental transfers in our analysis include both Federal and state grant-in-aid programs.

8. Statistical swing provides a convenient measure for quantifying the sensitivity of financial variables to changing circumstances. In this table, statistical swing represents the percent variation as social conditions shift from small-to-large dependent population ratios or as population densities shift from low to high and as economic conditions shift from the best conditions (high investment) to worst conditions (below-average investment). While the percentage change may appear small in some cases, nonetheless the amount of state and Federal aid involved is substantial.

Part II
Method and Analysis

2

Background

The research presented in this book was designed to examine empirically the linkages among different local economic, social, and structural conditions and municipal financial performance. To do so, a number of impediments that have been encountered by researchers of this issue in the past had to be overcome.

A principal difficulty facing researchers of municipal finance has been the lack of a comprehensive, consistent, and reliable financial data base. This is largely due to the variations in accounting procedures across cities and the nonavailability (noncollection) in many cities of major categories of financial information. Even when significant financial data are available, the inconsistency in treatment of this information among cities and the existence of overlapping jurisdictions have made meaningful comparative analysis of municipal financial performance exceedingly difficult.

We reasoned that the creation of a municipal financial data system would allow us to overcome limitations that had existed in earlier investigations. We overcame many of the troublesome problems of financial limitations and inconsistencies in the data by consulting the annual reports of individual cities, and unpublished information from the U.S. Bureau of the Census. As we continued building our data base, the number of financial variables analyzed was reduced due to certain remaining data constraints. The final result was a relatively comprehensive data base among 66 medium-to-large cities, and the accomplishment of our first research objective: enrichment of the municipal financial data base to allow comparisons among cities.

Another difficulty traditionally encountered by researchers has arisen from the use of economic, social, and structural variables as proxies for municipal financial variables. Specifically, such nonfinancial indicators as population decline and unemployment rate—rather than financial indicators such as debt and expenses—have been used to measure the fiscal condition of cities. Indeed, it is widely believed that there is a one-to-one relationship between socio-economic conditions and fiscal conditions.

The research challenge of this study was to reassess this relationship by examining empirically the combined and individual financial performance of cities in widely differing circumstances. Admittedly, the way in which variations in economic, social, and structural conditions affect municipal financial performance is extraordinarily complex. Nonetheless, all cities are buffeted by a range of economic, social, and structural forces that increase the demands for expenditures and, in turn, for revenue through a multiple cause-and-effect process. As the demands for public goods and services are met, municipal expenses must rise and ultimately be financed through the successful blending of tax, debt, and governmental transfers. Thus, the economic, social, and structural causes affect municipal expenditures which in turn affect the revenue side of the municipal budget. Gaining a better understanding of this cause and effect process constituted our second research objective.

A third research difficulty has been a conceptual framework needed to compare financial performance among cities with different economic, social, and structural conditions. For example, a simple correlation matrix of widely used key financial, economic, social, and structural variables—described in Appendix A—reveals that 93 percent of the correlation coefficients had at best a weak statistical relationship. (A correlation coefficient represents the degree of statistical association between two seemingly independent variables.) Indeed, in many cases, the relationship is actually random. This clearly suggests that when variables representing widely different economic, social, and structural conditions are indiscriminately mixed, it is extremely difficult to compare financial performance among cities.

A methodological framework was needed through which cities could be classified into relatively homogeneous economic, social, and structural clusters as a basis for studying the financial impact of change. We achieved this third objective by grouping the 66 cities into four clusters based on their level of investment and income in the private sector. Each economic cluster was then separated into two smaller clusters depending upon social conditions (for example, high versus low dependent population) and structural conditions (high versus low population density). This produced sixteen clusters that provided the basis for observing how changes in economic, social, and structural conditions affect municipal financial performance.

Of particular interest was the strong correspondence between these clusters and stages of city growth from early development to industrial maturity. This suggests that cities at roughly the same economic growth stage, with the same social and structural conditions, may be expected to make similar demands on the municipal financial structure.

As we describe the analysis undertaken to achieve our three objectives—enrichment of the municipal financial data base, conceptualization of the linkages between economic, social, and structural conditions and municipal financial performance, and the development of a methodology for classifying and analyzing cities based on their economic, social, and structural conditions—it will be helpful to bear in mind our four overall research steps:

Step 1: Collect economic, social, structural, and financial data for each of the 66 cities. Organize these data for each city, and create a consolidated computerized data system for ready access and ease of analysis.

Step 2: Analyze statistically the variables in the municipal financial data base for the 66 cities in order to select a Short List of Municipal Financial Performance Variables. This Short List represents the minimum number of performance variables that explain the maximum amount of municipal financial variance in the entire data base.

Step 3: Disaggregate statistically the variables in the Short List of Municipal Financial Performance Variables into relatively homogeneous municipal clusters in terms of their principal underlying economic, social, and structural conditions.

Step 4: Analyze linkages between economic, social, and structural conditions and municipal financial performance on a city-by-city basis. Gain a systematic understanding of how key indicators vary across the cities.

As our analysis progressed, we developed a working concept of fiscal stress. We reasoned that the concept of stress should provide a practical way of judging the rate at which a city's tax, debt, and expense rates approach outer boundaries—or sustainable financial limits—compared to cities with generally similar economic, social, and structural conditions.

We concluded that as cities begin to approach the outer limits, the number of expense and revenue trade-off options are greatly diminished. Should expenditure rates continue to outpace revenue capacity, financial disequilibrium would result. Although the precise determination of where financial limits begin is difficult to ascertain, the concept of limits does provide new insight into the empirical measurement of municipal fiscal stress.

Of the 66 cities in our data base, only 4 have financial patterns which place them in the zone of the limits, i.e., highest values of tax, debt, and expense rates for the overall sample. Therefore, we have concluded that almost all of the 66 cities in this survey have managed to balance financial capacity satisfactorily against local expenditures, given their particular economic, social, and structural conditions.

3 Creation of the Financial Data Base

One of the most important steps in this analysis was the creation of the financial data base. Historically, comparative analyses of municipal financial performance have been limited either by the nonavailability or noncomparability of financial data across cities. Not surprisingly, such factors can render statistical comparisons inadequate or inaccurate.

The first step in the data collection and refinement process was the gathering of all available statistical financial information on a targeted set of cities. Initially, we selected 120 cities, all with populations in excess of 50,000. The nation's ten largest cities, based on population, were excluded from the analysis on the grounds that their dominant financial shifts would tend to conceal important financial variations in the middle-sized cities. Indeed, there is enough evidence in the stock of economic literature to suggest that the largest cities are a qualitatively different group which should be analyzed separately.

Financial information for each city was collected from a number of sources: the U.S. Bureau of the Census municipal finance data tapes, Moody's Investors Service, and individual city annual reports. All data are for 1975, unless otherwise specified.[1]

Not all of the financial data collected were of direct relevance to a comparative analysis of municipal financial performance. What was needed was a standardized framework to organize and highlight certain aspects of the financial statements. The framework utilized for this study emphasized municipal flows of funds. Within this framework each city's financial indicators were systematically organized into five basic groupings. The groupings were based upon whether a variable deals with:

Current level and stability of operating surplus or deficit

Current liquidity of known financial resources

Ability to generate additional revenue either from own sources or from intergovernmental transfers

Ability to assume additional debt

Long-term capital requirements

We also determined that each city's financial statement should conform reasonably to Governmental Accounting, Auditing, and Financial Reporting

(GAAFR) standards published by the Municipal Finance Officers Association, 1968. The GAAFR condition provided additional rigor to the data collection.

This procedure identified the municipal financial data that would give us insight into the financial performance of cities.

A selection process reduced the initial target group of 120 cities to 66 and eliminated certain performance variables. Cities and variables were removed from the original lists due to inconsistencies, lack of accounting detail, or lack of availability. The resulting financial data base contained some one hundred financial performance variables for the 66 cities.

A comparison of these financial variables to our conceptual framework confirmed that we had a sufficient number of performance indicators in each major category for all of the 66 cities. This assured us that we had enough data to analyze municipal financial performance across the cities. Our procedures for data selection undoubtedly produced a slight bias in favor of better-managed cities, in that cities selected for this study had to have sufficient financial information available.

The next step was the selection of a manageable number of financial variables from the one hundred in the original financial data base.

The Short List of Municipal Financial Performance Variables

A number of well-established statistical techniques may be employed to select subgroups of variables from larger groups. In this analysis, we employed factor analysis to select the variables which tended to explain wide variations among the cities examined. Factor analysis is explicitly designed to cluster large numbers of highly dissimilar variables into factors representing similar or like behavior. Factor analysis differs from the more widely used statistical technique of regression analysis in that it does not attempt to explain statistical variation in a dependent variable by variations in a set of independent variables. Thus, regression analysis requires some *a priori* judgment as to which variables are independent and dependent. Some of the independent variables in regression analysis are usually rejected either on *a priori* grounds or because they appear to be statistically insignificant. Factor analysis, by contrast, retains the widest possible range of many relevant variables in a study. Thus, it can be used to systematically sort through variables from a large initial pool of data. It will select the variances that are quantifiably important and identify a manageable number of relatively homogeneous clusters which incorporate the key variables. An initial factor analysis using our entire financial data base yielded a set of 41 variables which were statistically significant. A second factor analysis was then performed on these 41 variables to further reduce the variables to a more manageable size.

The second factor analysis identified 22 financial variables that are the most statisticaly significant measures of financial performance among those derived for the 66 cities. These 22 financial variables capture the essential interrelations among all of the revenue, debt, and expense items contained in the data base. As such, they provide insight into the similarities and dissimilarities among the cities studied. Outlined in Table 3.1 are the 22 financial variables grouped into clusters that define the most explanatory characteristics of cities in the sample.

The appearance of ten variables in Factor 1 does not suggest unique significance to this factor relative to the others. The variables that cluster in any factor are there, first because of the high degree of inter-correlation, and second, because of their high degree of noncorrelation with variables in other factors. Although it is true that Factor 1 accounts for the greatest total factor variance (and each of the remaining factors has less explanatory power in terms of variance than the factors which precede it), we must note that the following four

Table 3.1
Statistically Significant Financial Performance Measures among the 66 Cities

Factor 1: *Current Expense Variables*

Current operating expenses per capita
Fire expenses per capita
Ratio of local taxes to personal income (tax effort)
Health expenses per capita (total from all sources)
Welfare expenses per capita (total from all sources)
Police expenses per capita
Local taxes per capita
Net health and hospital expenses per capita
Ratio of city full-time-equivalent employment to total local employment
City full-time-equivalent employment per capita

Factor 2: *Intergovernmental Transfer Variables*

Surplus to gross current operating expenses
Change in intergovernmental revenue as a percent of total local revenue
Ratio of revenue to total debt service

Factor 3: *Educational Expense Variables*

Education expenses per capita (total from all sources)
Net education expenses per capita
Average city employee annual income

Factor 4: *Municipal Debt Variables*

Total debt per capita
Municipal capital spending per capita, five-year average, 1971-75
Full-faith and credit debt per capita
Interest per capita

Factor 5: *Property Tax Variables*

Percent of property tax collected, 1975
Change in property tax collected, 1970-1975

factors are also important. Taken together, they constitute significant financial performance measures for judging the relative financial conditions of the 66 cities.

Factor 1 includes a relatively wide range of variables that emphasize the importance of current expense categories in municipal government. Note the compatibility of such variables as city employment and fire, police, and welfare expenditures. Thus, the first and most significant grouping of variables represents operating expenses. Education cost is notable by its absence from this factor. It shows up as a separate factor by itself (number 3), indicating that this cost is not only important in itself, but it behaves differently from other common municipal expenses.

Factor 2 is a set of variables that describes the governmental transfer role in municipal revenue. In our analysis, both Federal and state transfers are grouped together. The surplus to gross operating expenditures ratio and, to a greater extent, revenue to debt service ratio, also appear in this factor because of their close correspondence to revenue flows from outside sources. Municipalities are becoming increasingly dependent upon revenue transfers from Federal and state government. Therefore, it is not surprising that our statistical procedures identify these as a separate factor.

Factor 3 is a grouping of education expenses. In all of the factor analyses conducted in the project, variation in education expenditures was in a separate factor.

Factor 4 represents the grouping of municipal debt. Like the education expenditure grouping, it consistently appears to be homogeneous. Note the presence of the capital spending and interest variables with the two debt variables.

Factor 5 appears to be the grouping of financial variables that are most commonly associated with fiscal strain — especially the property tax variables.

A final comment may be made about the financial variables that do not appear to be statistically significant across the 66 cities. These are:

Short-term debt to cash and investments

Property tax revenue to total tax revenue

Sewage and sanitation expenditures per capita

General funds surplus to expenditures

Percent of property taxes collected in 1970

Net housing and urban renewal expenditures per capita

General cash flow per capita.

The fact that these financial variables were statistically insignificant in explaining financial variance across the 66 cities implies that the variables are poor estimators of the common variances across the cities. Some or all of them may be of significance in interpreting individual municipal financial characteristics or performance in some of the cities, but in the aggregate they are not.

The last step in the construction of our financial data base was the selection of the Short List of Municipal Financial Performance Variables. The concept of developing a Short List of performance measures is well known in empirical economic analysis, having its origins in the cyclical performance analyses of the National Bureau of Economic Research. Accordingly, we have applied this concept to financial variables. The Short List is made up of a relatively small number of variables that tend to provide substantial insight into an even larger set of data from which they are drawn. This selection process combined the results of the previous factor analyses with a number of additional criteria and finally with our own judgment. The criteria we employed were:

High score in the factor analyses

Accounting consistency

Availability

Relevance to determination of municipal financial policy

Representative of significant financial areas

The 13 variables selected for the Short List were:

Revenue

Ratio of local taxes to personal income

Local taxes per capita

Intergovernmental revenue as a percent of total local revenue

Debt

Total debt per capita

Interest per capita

Municipal capital spending per capita, five-year average, 1971-75

Expense

Fire expenses per capita

Education expenses per capita

Health expenses per capita

Welfare expenses per capita

Ratio of city full-time-equivalent employment to total local employment

Average city employee annual income

Current operating expenses per capita

Data Sources for the Short List Variables

Because the variables in the Short List play a critical role in our analysis, it is necessary to describe each of them and their data sources in detail. Note that all variables have been adjusted—by expressing them in per capita or ratio terms—to facilitate comparisons across the 66 cities.

Ratio of Local Taxes to Personal Income (Tax Effort)

The tax effort variable measures the resource demands placed by the municipality on its citizens relative to their ability to pay. Taxes consist of property, sales, gross receipts, and any other levies imposed by the city on individuals and businesses for all purposes. This number does not include fees, utility revenue, liquor store revenue, or employer and employee assessments for retirement and social insurance. Any state-imposed taxes are classified as intergovernmental revenue. To insure that this tax variable was comparable between cities with municipal school districts and those with regional ones, taxes collected by independent districts were obtained from unpublished Census Bureau data and allocated to the city. The allocation was based on population percentages. Personal income is the total income for the city as provided in the U.S. Bureau of the Census County and City Data Book and Current Population Reports.

Local Taxes per Capita

The taxes in this variable are defined as above, and the population figure is taken from U.S. Bureau of the Census data. This variable represents the dollars of taxation which the average citizen of a municipality has paid. It is not necessarily an indicator of strain even if it is large, since no measure of ability to pay has been included. However, it is useful in comparing relative tax burdens for the cities in our survey.

Intergovernmental Revenue as a
Percent of Total Local Revenue

This variable is composed entirely of Census Bureau data. The denominator, general revenue, is all city revenue except utility revenue and employee retirement or other insurance trust revenue. Included are all tax collections and intergovernmental revenue.

Intergovernmental revenue is the amounts received from other governments in the form of shared revenues and grants-in-aid, as reimbursements for performance of general government functions and specific services for the paying government (for example, care of prisoners or contractual research), or in lieu of taxes. It excludes amounts received from other governments for sale of property, commodities, and utility services. All intergovernmental revenue is classified as general revenue.

This variable shows the portion of a city's total general fund revenue which comes from state and Federal transfers (including revenue sharing) as well as local government sources of revenue outside the municipal tax base. This variable indicates the degree to which a city depends on outside resources.

Total Debt per Capita

This variable is made up of all long-term debt outstanding (general obligation revenue and special assessment), both guaranteed and nonguaranteed, plus short-term debt outstanding. This debt total includes Redevelopment Housing Authority debt where applicable, but excludes long-term debt issued in support of municipal utilities. Again, to insure comparability of this variable among cities with and without independent school districts, we added the debt of independent school districts based on a population percentage allocation. The variable measures the level of future commitment which has been, on average, undertaken by each city. The comparison of this variable among the cities in our sample also indicates the ability of the city to undertake additional debt obligations.

Interest per Capita

This variable is the total current interest expense generated by the debt burden described above. This variable represents a portion of the current expense burden imposed by the level of future commitment which the city has undertaken.

Municipal Capital Spending per Capita,
Five-Year Average, 1971-75

This variable is an average general capital expenditure for the years 1971 through 1975 (all city expenditures other than the specifically enumerated kinds of expenditure classified as utility expenditure, liquor store expenditure, and employee retirement or other insurance trust expenditure), except for education expenses. The five-year average was used in order to smooth out any special capital expenditures that may have occurred in a single year. It is made up of data from both the Census Bureau and the individual annual reports and is divided by the city's average population over the five-year period. Since in many respects education is a stand-alone item, we felt this variable was more meaningful with education excluded. This variable allows us to compare how adequately cities in our survey have provided for the maintenance and renewal of their capital stock and what might be required in the future.

Fire Expenses per Capita

This variable is the total noncapital expenditure made by the city for fire protection, divided by the city population. It includes expenditures for city fire-fighting organizations and their auxiliary services, inspection for fire hazards, and other fire prevention activities. Also included is the cost of fire-fighting facilities, such as fire hydrants and water—furnished by other agencies of the city government.

Education Expenses per Capita
(Total from All Sources)

This variable is the total noncapital expenditure made by the city for education, divided by the city population. Educational expenditures are based on Census Bureau data and include costs for schools and other educational facilities and services. Local school expenses include city-operated elementary and secondary schools and other educational institutions (other than higher education) and intergovernmental expenditures for education, payments to private institutions, and special educational programs. Expenses of city-operated local schools include administration and supervision of the school system and related school-administered facilities and services such as public transportation, school health and recreational programs, school lunch programs, and school libraries.

One of our major concerns was comparability of the education, tax, debt, and expense variables between cities with independent, regional, or county-dependent school districts and those without such districts. To resolve this problem, detailed unpublished survey forms were obtained from the Census Bureau. Using the portion of the school district's population which resided in the city, divided by the total population of the school district, we were able to allocate these tax, debt, and expense values to the city proper. In our statistical analysis, all variables associated with education were comprised of the values taken from the Census Bureau plus the values calculated by our allocation process.

Health Expenses per Capita
(Total from All Sources)

This variable is the total gross noncapital expenditure made by the city for health including intergovernmental transfers divided by the city population. Health expenditures are based on Census Bureau data and encompass all public health activity costs except hospital care. This includes environmental health activities such as health regulation and inspection, water and air pollution control, mosquito control, and inspection of food handling establishments. Activities also included are public health nursing, collection of vital statistics, and other services performed directly by the public health department. Specifically excluded are payments made under public welfare programs.

Welfare Expenses per Capita
(Total from All Sources)

This variable is the total noncapital expenditure made by the city for welfare, divided by the city population. This variable is a composite of variables taken from the Census Bureau and consists of support of and assistance to persons contingent upon their need as deemed by the appropriate state and local authorities. It excludes pensions to former employees and other benefits not contingent on need. Since the welfare system for some municipalities is funded at the state or county level, this variable's value may be zero in some cases. In isolated cases, revenues exceed expenditures for the selected period. Expenditures under this heading include: cash assistance paid directly to needy persons under categorical programs (old age assistance, aid to families with dependent children, aid to the blind, and aid to the disabled) and under any other welfare programs (general relief, home relief, poor relief); vendor payments made directly to private purveyors for medical care, hospital care, burials, and other commodities and services provided under welfare programs; and provision and operation by the city of welfare institutions. Other public welfare expenditures include city payments to other nonmunicipal governments for welfare purposes, amounts for administration, support of private welfare agencies (including nursing homes), and other public welfare services (foster care). Health and hospital services provided directly by the city through its own hospitals and health agencies, and any payments to other governments for such purposes, are included under those headings rather than here.

Ratio of City Full-Time-Equivalent Employment to Total Local Employment

This ratio variable is the total number of full-time-equivalent employees for the city in 1970 (those employed only by the city government, excluding all Federal and state agencies), divided by the private and public employment of those residing in the city. All data for this variable are taken from the Census Bureau County and City Data Book. Employment is defined as employed civilians who were earlier (a) "at work"—those who did any work at all as paid employees or in their own business or profession, or on their own farm, or who worked fifteen hours or more as unpaid workers on a family farm or in a family business; or (b) were "with a job but not at work"—those who did not work during the reference week but had jobs or businesses from which they were temporarily absent due to illness, bad weather, industrial dispute, vacation, or other reasons. Excluded are persons whose only activity consisted of work around the house or volunteer work for religious, charitable, and similar organizations. Additionally, no CETA workers are included. The variable gives an indication of the size of municipal government relative to the total employment base of a city.

Average City Employee Annual Income

This variable is the average annual salary received by each municipal employee. The denominator is full-time-equivalent employment as defined above and the numerator is the total gross salary paid to all employees of the city and its agencies—regular, temporary, full-time, and part-time. This variable also includes salaries of municipal utility employees.

Current Operating Expenses per Capita

This variable is the total noncapital general expenditures of the city (including current expenses funded from general revenue sharing), less revenues received from Federal, state, and other local governments for specific purposes. Revenues from hospital, housing, and urban renewal charges collected by the city are also removed. It also excludes miscellaneous revenues such as parking fees. This variable is an overall indicator of the expenses typically supported directly by taxation of the citizens.

Summary

It will be helpful to summarize at this point by emphasizing what we accomplished thus far in the analysis: namely, the creation of a Short List of Municipal Financial Performance Variables for the 66 cities. This Short List is statistically significant—it represents the cluster of variables that must be given considerable weight in interpreting municipal fiscal conditions. The Short List is also practical in that it is composed of a manageable number of variables that can be easily manipulated, described, and analyzed. Our principal conclusion in arriving at this Short List is that sufficient data do exist for meaningful analysis. However, as we will describe in the following section, there is considerable room for improvement.

The Need for Improved Municipal Financial Reporting

In constructing the financial data base, it became apparent that there was a need in some areas for additional or improved data. Had these data been available, it would have expanded the scope of our analysis. Nonetheless, there was sufficient data available for meaningful analysis.

Data problems fell broadly into three categories: (1) lack of detail on published data, (2) inconsistent data, and (3) unavailable data. In the first category, our solution to the problem insofar as a solution was possible, was to obtain unpublished and detailed data from the U.S. Bureau of the Census, municipal financial reports, and annual reports for the individual cities.

In the second category are those items which were available but which were either inconsistent or noncomparable among our 66 cities due to variations in accounting practices. In the third category are unavailable data, and here we were unable to close any of the gaps.

Published Data Lacking in Detail

The major problem stemming from the lack of detail in the financial data base was the absence of a breakdown in the tax revenue sources: residential versus corporate. This reduced the value of such indicators as property tax revenue per capita for determining the tax burden on individual citizens. Additionally, any attempt at comparisons, such as tax revenues to value added or measures of corporate tax burden, is difficult. A partial solution to this problem could have been developed by obtaining detailed information from city assessors and tax collectors, but this was beyond the scope of our study.

Expenditures offered several problems. In most cases, capital expenditures could not be traced back to the actual revenue source. Conversely, long-term debt issues could not be identified with the proper expenditure item. Thus, no real evaluation of the uses of the debt could be made based on new construction, renovation, maintenance, or even operating expense. With no way to identify revenue sources for these capital expenditures, the question of what portion of these expenditures was actually supported by current revenue was unanswerable. Obviously, where cities had established enterprise or special-revenue funds, we were able to avoid this problem, but this was not always the case. To compound this problem, we felt that it was frequently unclear whether many maintenance-related operating expenses should not, in fact, have been classified as capital rather than current expenditures. The net result of these expenditure problems is that we cannot comment either on a city's ability to match asset versus liability maturities on its balance sheet or on the efficiency of a city's true capital expenditure program.

Another major deficiency in the expenditure data was that spending for programs mandated by a higher level of government was often inseparable from spending for services locally authorized. Thus, the adequacy of intergovernmental transfers to cover mandated expenses could not be determined.[2] The information provided by the unpublished census data and the annual reports was not consistently detailed enough to allow us to calculate these ratios.

Short-term debt and pension liabilities were also troublesome. Since short-term debt was not broken down into categories such as tax anticipation notes or bond anticipation notes, a true picture of a city's long-term liabilities was unclear. The annual reports did not consistently provide enough detail to resolve this problem. Consequently, it was difficult to determine what portion of the short-term debt was actually funding current operations and might have been rolled over for several years.

Pension liabilities were included only in the annual reports of a few cities in our study. When present, it was sometimes unclear whether they were an actuarial present value or total future cost. Other cities simply showed current year pension expenditures on a pay-as-you-go basis. A few cities had not even broken this out as a separate expense item. Comparability was further impaired because some of the cities participated in regional or state pension systems. We were finally forced to drop this variable from our analysis. It is very important, however, that future studies pay attention to pension liabilities, which are becoming increasingly important to the financial condition of cities.[3]

Our last major problem with assets concerns an item which does not actually appear on the balance sheet: market value of taxable property. Typically, if this item is available, it is based on a sample of recent market transactions. Since industrial property tends to change hands infrequently, this number is understated. Additionally, no breakdown is given between individual versus corporate ownership of this property, so we have no insight into the makeup of the tax base. Another item which would be of interest is the amount of land and property in the city which is not subject to taxation. Thus, a city with a high number of higher education institutions or churches cannot be sufficiently distinguished from one with a heavy industrial or private residence base. Again, had the scope of our study been greatly increased, some of this information could have been gathered from local assessors and tax collectors.[4]

Inconsistent Data

The major overall problem of data consistency lay in distinguishing between cash and accrual data. Historically, cities have employed cash-basis accounting, but in recent years there has been a clear trend to accrual accounting. The latter matches more accurately expense with revenue. For data not obtained from the Census Bureau, we identified how financial information was treated for a particular fund through the annual reports to improve consistency. In the data base, those cities which most exactly conformed to GAAFR were easier to deal with.

A problem in collecting estimates of long-term debt arose from our inability to identify the uses of the revenue derived from the debt sale. Long-term debt was complicated by the existence of overlapping liabilities generated by entities such as the state, an independent school district, or the county. We treated the independent school district overlap problem by allocating not only the long-term debt but also all other financial variable values obtained from unpublished census data based on population percentages. The annual reports for the individual cities were also used to obtain detail on other overlapping liabilities.

Unavailable Data

As one would expect, data about long-term assets for our sample cities were nonexistent. There is no accounting for capital consumption or depreciation of fixed assets in the public sector. Consequently, we had no way of determining the age of a city's capital stock or possible requirements for new plant and equipment. Short-term investments also posed a problem because we could not determine the sources of the cash. Invested proceeds from a bond offering made early to take advantage of market conditions or current authorization were indistinguishable from other cash flow contributors. Although some cities presented this information in their annual reports, we had insufficient data to analyze this issue.

In many cases, information about the authorized but unissued portion of long-term debt was not available. Thus the ease (or difficulty, as in the case of those cities which had reached their authorized limit) with which additional debt could be floated could not be assessed.

Other Data Problems

An additional data problem was of a nonfinancial nature—the population number used to adjust the financial variables. Since many cities have a large commuter segment in the work force, such items as tax revenue per capita do not truly reflect the burden on the citizens. Similarly, expense items, such as sanitation expenditures per capita, reflect only partially the amount of services provided to the citizens. We felt that by excluding the largest and most highly agglomerated cities, we could improve upon, although not completely resolve, this problem.

Another statistical problem that requires brief comment concerns a city's taxing and spending authority. Unquestionably, there are major variations among municipalities in their jurisdictional boundaries. The larger the municipality's base, the greater the likelihood that municipal operating statements and balance sheets will encompass the totality of the city's economic base activities. On the other hand, small or narrowly defined legal jurisdictions found in some states can only encompass a small portion of the total urban or metropolitan area. This long-standing problem of untangling municipal spillovers in taxing and spending effects should be noted but will most certainly go unresolved for some time to come.

We may summarize by noting that, although there is a range of statistical and accounting problems associated with the measurement of municipal financial performance, data limitations simply reduced the scope of our analysis. Thus the thrust of our analysis was to focus on those variables which were both statistically significant and reliable among all 66 cities.

Notes

1. Computation of financial ratios made use of estimated July 1, 1975 population and 1974 per capita income obtained from the U.S. Department of Commerce, Bureau of the Census, Current Population Reports, series P-25, May 1977.

2. The National Science Foundation has recently initiated a project to analyze whether state mandated programs cause municipalities to incur costs which are not adequately borne by intermunicipal transfers. A small number of municipalities in California and New Jersey are being examined.

3. The U.S. Department of Housing and Urban Development has recently funded a large study of municipal pension systems, which is being carried out by the Urban Institute. See also the recent American Enterprise Institute study of the New York City pension system, which estimates that the City's contributions will have to rise substantially if the system is to become actuarially sound,

even though retirement costs already consume approximately 40 percent of the city's tax levy.

4. A recent (1978) study of tax exempt property in cities by William A. McEachern, "Tax Exempt Property and Tax Capitalization in Central Cities" indicates that tax exemption in high property tax cities may have a cumulatively adverse effect on the cities' fiscal situation. New England Business and Economic Conference, October 13, 1978.

4

The Linkages between Economic, Social, and Structural Conditions and Financial Performance: A Methodological Framework

The manner in which variations in real-world social, economic, and structural conditions affect municipal financial performance is extraordinarily complex. This is the case because no two municipal economies develop in exactly the same way: some local economies are growing, while others are maturing or declining. Complexity also results from the wide range of municipal expenditure responses to the changing demand for public goods and services, to management control, and to variations in the taxing and spending patterns at different levels of government.

All of these factors make it exceedingly difficult to gain a clear understanding of the cause and effect relationships between nonfinancial conditions and municipal financial performance. Nonetheless, if meaningful statistical analysis is to be undertaken, the myriad factors affecting a municipality's financial performance have to be grouped into manageable categories. Three types of real-world forces—economic, social, and structural—account for the major impacts on a municipality's financial performance. A brief comment on each of these forces will be helpful in building a foundation for the subsequent analyses.

Economic conditions in a municipality reflect the amount of private sector investment in plant, equipment, and commercial structures. Also included within this category are such factors as incomes and their distribution among the citizenry, the occupational structure of the private labor market, and the age composition of the resident population.

Private sector capital spending is the driving force that produces economic growth. Whenever a city is growing rapidly, new jobs are being created, and when income is rising, expanding investment will be evident. Conversely, when industrial maturity is reached, private sector capital formation slows down. ("Maturing" and "aging" will continue to be used interchangeably in this study.) Economic conditions—especially investment—have the most significant impact on a city's financial performance inasmuch as they determine its growth path. On the other hand, economic determinants cannot be judged alone because they are influenced by social and structural conditions.

Social conditions in a municipality are linked to economic conditions. In one sense, they can be described as the consequences of economic growth. For

51

example, rapid private sector investment in manufacturing may induce a lower unemployment rate and the reduction of poverty among those who were previously unemployed. The condition of a municipality's housing stock as well as the relative share of minority residents are also important variables that describe or reflect the municipality's social conditions.

In another sense, social conditions include a wide range of circumstances that are distinct from economic conditions and can in themselves induce change. Changes in social conditions can force changes in the level and mix of public services. For example, the deterioration of the housing stock will lead to demands for increased municipal fire expenditures, and increases in unemployment put pressure on the municipality to provide more social services.

While adverse social conditions provide a disincentive for investment, the elimination of unfavorable social conditions will not necessarily mean that new investment will flow into the city. Business investment decisions are made on the basis of a wide range of underlying cost-price factors. Thus, we may surmise that social conditions in themselves are important, but they must be integrated into the private investment equation along with other factors, including structural conditions.

Structural conditions include a relatively wide range of factors that delimit the taxing and spending parameters for a particular city as well as its relationship with contiguous cities and higher levels of government. A structural factor is perhaps best described in terms of the city's jurisdictional boundaries. Structural factors are vitally important because the spatial dimensions of economic activity (especially investment) do not necessarily coincide, or overlap, with a municipality's jurisdictional boundaries. Furthermore, investment shifts from one city to another can produce dramatic changes in a municipality's tax base. Some specific structural conditions are well known: number of square miles in the city, annexation constraints, and population density.

We may summarize at this point by reiterating that the range of financial responses to economic, social, and structural forces by municipal officials is extremely varied and complex. This complexity is easy to appreciate when one calculates a simple correlation matrix among economic, social, structural, and financial variables. We produced the matrix for the Short List of Financial Variables and 11 economic, social, and structural variables across the 66 cities. The detailed results are discussed in Appendix A, but it is worth noting that among 132 correlation coefficients, 123—93 percent—had at best only a weak statistical relationship or one that should be more properly defined as random. This demonstrates rather clearly that economic, social, structural, and financial variables cannot be indiscriminately mixed.

The Methodological Framework Conceptualized

What was clearly needed was a methodological framework that permitted the classification of the 66 cities into relatively homogeneous economic, social, and structural clusters in order to be able to study the impact of economic, social, and structural changes on the performance of the financial variables in the Short List. The methodological framework we developed contained 16 clusters. Four economic clusters were utilized, enabling us to group cities on the basis of their level of private sector investment and income. Each economic cluster was then disaggregated into smaller clusters depending upon social conditions (high versus low dependent population) and structural conditions (high versus low population density). Thus, the 16 clusters describe a wide range of combinations of economic and social, or economic and structural conditions that are homogeneous in themselves, but heterogeneous with respect to each other. They provide a manageable, theoretically satisfactory way to analyze municipal financial performance across cities with relatively similar economic, social, and structural conditions. This specific methodological framework is described in Table 4.1.

Table 4.1
The Methodological Framework for Classifying Economic, Social, and Structural Conditions into 16 Clusters

Economic Conditions	Social Conditions	Structural Conditions
High private investment and high income	Large dependent population	
	Small dependent population	
		High population density
		Low population density
Above-average private investment and income	Large dependent population	
	Small dependent population	
		High population density
		Low population density
Average private investment and income	Large dependent population	
	Small dependent population	
		High population density
		Low population density
Below-average private investment and income	Large dependent population	
	Small dependent population	
		High population density
		Low population density

The next step was the selection of the economic, social, and structural variables to allocate the 66 cities into the 16 clusters. In passing, it should be noted that we identified these variables through two statistical techniques—factor analysis of more than 100 socio-economic variables across the sample cities as well as economic base theory.

Economic Conditions: Private
Investment and Income

The first set of variables describes the economic condition of a city:

Change in population

Percent of change in single-family housing starts

Manufacturing capital spending

Change in manufacturing employment ratio

Percent change in manufacturing capital spending

Median family income

The economic variables give primary emphasis to private-sector investment-related variables such as manufacturing capital spending and private sector housing investment. The level of median family income, when added to the investment variables, provided additional statistical refinement because of its analytical importance as a measure of the overall economic condition of a city. Finally, the percentage of change in population is included because population changes are important indicators of overall municipal growth.

The consequences of these economic variables for municipal finance are obvious. An economically sound and growing economy provides revenue growth while simultaneously taking pressure off the expense side of the budget by providing job opportunities to population groups that could otherwise become heavily dependent on municipal social services.

Social Conditions: Dependent Population
and Related Characteristics

A second set of variables was used to describe a wide range of social conditions found in different cities:

Percent minority population

Percent families below low-income level

Unemployment rate

Percent of pre-1939 housing stock

These four variables are clearly distinguishable from those in the economic cluster because they represent the social consequences of economic growth and investment. They are also different because they describe the demands of the service-dependent population for public goods and services—demands that are placed directly on the expenditure side of the municipal budget.

Structural Conditions:
Population Density

The final category employs only a single variable to describe the structural or jurisdictional constraints on a municipality's economic and fiscal base: population density. This variable could possibly have been used as well to provide insight into social conditions in a municipality. For example, crowded living conditions are positively associated with high population densities and inversely related to single-family housing rates. But we chose it as a variable to differentiate cities along structural lines for other reasons. We were specifically interested in a variable that would reflect variations in the tax base, thus providing insight into the extent to which annexation policies have or have not altered the size of the local economic base. The declining cities of the Northeast are of much smaller size—hence greater density—than their Southern and Western counterparts, and as will be seen in subsequent analyses, these spatial considerations are highly relevant to municipal financial performance.[1]

Ultimate determination, or classification, of a city into any one of the four economic clusters was accomplished through the calculation of Z-scores. Z-scoring is a well-established technique for classifying differences among sample data through the systematic statistical manipulation of the deviations from the mean for each of the individual economic variables. As is standard procedure, the specific variances in the economic variables for each of the 66 cities were subtracted from the mean value for each variable and normalized (divided) by the standard deviation for each variable for all 66 cities. By restating each variable in terms of its Z-score, differences due to absolute magnitude are eliminated. For example, although manufacturing capital spending and median family income may have had significantly different means and standard deviations, once normalized, two data points that are one standard deviation from the mean of each variable would have the same value. After the individual Z-scores were calculated for the six economic variables, the values were summed algebraically, positive signs indicating an aggregate score greater than the sample mean. The four economic clusters were then created wherever statistical discontinuities, or breaks, in the algebraically summed arrays occurred. Once the cities had been assigned to the four economic clusters, the city splits could be made in terms of high or low social conditions, as well as high or low population densities. These classifications were also determined on the basis of the Z-scores for the social and structural variables within the four economic clusters. The specific city-by-city classifications are shown in Table 4.2.

Each of the four economic clusters of cities in Table 4.2—high investment, above-average investment, average investment, and below-average investment— reflected, to a significant extent, the stage of growth of its component cities. For example, the older, industrialized cities in the data base appear to be grouped in the average and below-average clusters, while the high-investment cluster is dominated by the young, rapidly growing cities. As the analysis progressed, an adjustment was required in our methodology to reflect stage of growth, or age of industrialization. This adjustment enabled us to differentiate with greater precision the effects of aging on municipal financial performance among two quite different kinds of cities grouped in the same economic cluster: older cities with relatively low investment levels due to economic decline and young cities with low investment levels because they are just beginning to industrialize. Before describing the way in which economic aging was integrated into the methodology, it will be worthwhile to review briefly the manner in which economic growth takes place at the municipal level.

Stages of Industrial Aging—
Theoretical Considerations

The broad guidelines of city growth are fairly well understood. Basic to the growth of a city is its capacity for stimulating private-sector capital spending among existing and new industries. Each city has an internal environment that tends to favor certain industrial specialties. Growth impulses, however, come largely from the outside economy in the form of demands on the industrial specialties existing in the city's economic base. The nature of these specialties— for instance, heavy manufacturing or high-technology industrial specialization— the competing sources among them, and the changes in the structure of demand determine in large measure the pattern and extent of city growth.

In all cities, the economic capacity, or resources, is dissimilar, and the external growth impulses are different for each resource or industrial specialization. However, as cities develop, noticeable industrial and economic similarities are evident. Cities with growing economies will eventually pass through a threshold beyond their initial industry-building phase. Cities with older economies will ultimately reach a mature phase of industrialization. To some this has meant economic stagnation, but others have renewed or rebuilt portions of their economic base.

A city typically follows a pattern of increasing-to-decreasing private-sector

Table 4.2
The Classification of the 66 Cities into Economic and Industrial Age Clusters

	Stage of Industrialization		
	Old Industrialized	*Industrially Maturing*	*Young Industrial Growth*
High private investment and income cities:			
Hollywood			•
Jacksonville			•
Bloomington			•
Irving			•
Indianapolis			•
Baton Rouge			•
Denver			•
Tempe			•
Phoenix			•
Above-average private investment and income cities:			
Kansas City			•
Stamford			•
Decatur			•
Madison			•
Rochester			•
Fort Worth			•
Omaha			•
Grand Rapids			•
Seattle		•	
Milwaukee		•	
Daly City			•
Evanston			•
Average private investment and income cities:			
Port Arthur			•
West Palm Beach			•
Duluth		•	
Mobile		•	
San Angelo			•
Amarillo			•
Little Rock			•
Topeka			•
Greensboro			•
Montgomery			•
Eugene			•
Lincoln			•
Wichita			•
Pueblo			•
Worcester	•		
Pasadena		•	
Springfield		•	
Louisville		•	
Dayton		•	

Table 4.2 continued

	Stage of Industrialization		
	Old Indus-trialized	*Industrially Maturing*	*Young Industrial Growth*
Syracuse		•	
Minneapolis		•	
Pittsburgh		•	
Bridgeport	•		
Baltimore	•		
Boston	•		
Cambridge	•		
Below-average private investment and income cities:			
Galveston			•
Salt Lake City			•
Albuquerque			•
New Orleans		•	
Jackson			•
Tucson			•
Tampa			•
Spokane		•	
Austin			•
Atlanta			•
St. Petersburg			•
Fresno			•
Richmond			•
Savannah			•
Long Beach			•
New Haven	•		
Hartford	•		
Buffalo	•		
Trenton	•		

investment, especially in manufacturing capital spending. Cities in their early growth stages generally experience rapid and extensive private-sector investment as well as substantial population in-migration. In sharp contrast, the most obvious characteristics of cities passing into the stage of economic, or industrial, maturity is the sustained loss of manufacturing employment. Manufacturing firms leave the cities largely because the costs of operating a manufacturing firm are generally less in the suburbs and rural areas.

As manufacturing decline accelerates, it soon leads to declines in the total municipal population. The compounded loss of prime manufacturing jobs and total population can have a significant adverse impact on the city's tax base, the citizenry's demand for government services, and the general well-being of the entire community. This, in turn, can lead to a financial disequilibrium between a city's underlying economic resources and the demands for public goods and services.

This line of reasoning takes on a special dimension when the spatial location of industry is considered; that is, there are significant regional variations in the cost-price structure of production that induce the migration of industry. The upper ranges in the cost of doing business are now concentrated in the fully developed, or more mature, regions and cities in the country—specifically the Northeast and the Great Lakes regions. Thus, there is an easily observed process of industry filtration from economically more mature cities to their contiguous suburbs and rural areas as well as to the less industrialized parts of the country.

Stages of Industrial Aging—
Methodological Considerations

There is a strong correspondence but not a precise fit between the four economic clusters in our classificatory scheme and the economic stages of development. Several factors account for the differences. First, a city can "buck" the economic aging process to some extent through successful renewal strategies. In such a case, the city would have been placed in a more favorable investment and income cluster than its stage of growth would warrant. Conversely, an industrially young city may have adopted policies which discourage private sector investment, thus placing it in a lower investment cluster. Second, several clusters (e.g., below-average investment) capture cities going in opposite directions of growth; that is, those just beginning to generate significant levels of private investment and those experiencing declining investment. Both may have, for a period of time, relatively similar investment levels.

As we attempted to incorporate the process of economic aging into our methodology, the differentiation of cities posed special problems that could not be handled through the Z-scores. Rather than judgmentally classify the cities by stage of growth or decline, we decided to employ the following empirical definitions:

Old industrialized—Cities in which manufacturing employment has declined in two consecutive periods, 1954-1967 and 1967-1972, in which the rate of decline in manufacturing employment accelerated in the second period; and in which population declined in two periods, 1950-1960 and 1960-1970. The following nine cities were classified in this cluster:

Bridgeport	Cambridge
Hartford	Worcester
New Haven	Trenton

Baltimore   Buffalo
Boston

Industrially maturing—Cities in which manufacturing employment declined in both the first and second periods or the second period alone; in which population declined in the period 1960-1970; and in which there was no acceleration in the rate of decline in manufacturing employment. The following 13 cities were determined to be in this category:

Dayton   Mobile
Pittsburgh   Pasadena
Seattle   Louisville
Spokane   New Orleans
Milwaukee   Springfield
Minneapolis   Duluth
                                 Syracuse

Young industrial growth—Cities in which both manufacturing employment and population were expanding in both of the periods analyzed. The remaining 44 cities were classified in this cluster.

Using these empirical definitions of stage of growth or decline, we determined the classification for cities in each of the economic clusters, as shown in Table 4.2.

Note specifically that only within the high investment and income cluster does the economic classification fit precisely with the stage of city growth. As expected, in the average and below-average investment and income clusters, there are cities classified in all three industrial age groups. This results from similar levels of low investment in old industrialized cities that have completed their development cycle and young cities that are just beginning to develop industrially. In the subsequent analyses, care is always taken within the economic clusters to separate these cities by their industrial age.

Using the Framework

The methodological framework discussed in this chapter will be used in the subsequent analyses in a number of ways. First, we will examine the aggregate performance of the financial variables on our Short List across the four economic clusters and their social and structural splits. After that discussion, we will analyze the financial performance of individual cities within each of the economic clusters, observing how changes in economic conditions—including the process of industrial aging—influence financial performance, as social and structural conditions vary.

As we examine cities individually, we will consider the impact of two additional forces that account for at least some of the variations across cities: geographic location and population size. Finally, we have included a description of the largest employers for each city as an indication of industry mix. However, no specific attempt was made to integrate this information into the statistical and methodological framework employed in this study.

In short, we are attempting to provide a workable methodology to identify relatively homogeneous economic, social, and structural conditions and relate these conditions to municipal financial performance. We may now turn our attention to the analysis across all 16 clusters.

Note

1. Norton, Robert, "City Life Cycles and American Urban Policy," Ph.D. Dissertation, Woodrow Wilson School, Princeton University, 1976. This study shows that annexation capability, density, and cost of government are significantly and systematically interrelated.

5 Analysis of Municipal Financial Performance across All 16 Clusters

In this stage of the analysis, we calculated the statistical means for each of the 13 financial variables on the Short List within each of the 16 clusters and for all 66 cities. Again our aim was to provide more insight into the linkages between the variations in economic, social, and structural conditions and municipal financial performance. Tables 5.1 and 5.2 show these means. The statistical disaggregation shown in these tables follows from the preceding framework and reduces economic, social, and structural change into logically consistent categories.

A brief comment is in order concerning the number of individual cities in each cluster. Although 66 cities would appear to provide a sample of sufficient magnitude for disaggregation into the clusters, this was not the case in every instance. Six of the clusters have a large number of cities. The maximum is 15 cities in the average private investment and income, low-population-density city cluster. Others are less adequate subsamples, especially those that contain five or fewer cities. These differences should be noted, because the larger the number of cities in any particular cluster, the more representative will be the observations derived from it.

Taxes

Overall, a clear pattern of variation is apparent between cities' economic-social-structural conditions and their tax burdens. Shown in Table 5.3 are the absolute values and the percentage changes in tax effort (local tax/personal income) and taxes per capita, comparing "best vs. worst" and "large vs. small" cases along the social and economic dimensions indicated.[1]

These variations show clearly that when worsening economic conditions are coupled with a shift to higher population density there is a dramatic rise in tax effort and taxes per capita. Furthermore, this shift from low to high population density and from best to worst economic conditions pushes the tax effort up nearly four times as much as the shift from small to large dependent population. This is an important finding that will be reinforced throughout many of the subsequent analyses; namely, that shifting structural conditions appear to have a greater impact on municipal financial performance than do changing social conditions.

Table 5.1
Variations in Structural and Economic Conditions: The Statistical Means

	Low Population Density				High Population Density					
	High Private Investment and Income	Above-Average Private Investment and Income	Average Private Investment and Income	Below-Average Private Investment and Income	High Private Investment and Income	Above-Average Private Investment and Income	Average Private Investment and Income	Below-Average Private Investment and Income	66 Cities Mean	Standard Deviation for All 66 Cities
Revenue:										
Ratio of local taxes to personal income	4.44%	5.46%	4.77%	4.97%	5.60%	5.58%	7.18%	8.55%	5.65%	2.26%
Local taxes per capita	$223.76	$289.99	$220.18	$218.73	$283.44	$298.86	$327.95	$360.00	$265.02	$106.41
Intergovernmental revenue as a percent of total local revenue	30.40%	29.90%	30.10%	35.90%	38.30%	37.60%	39.80%	37.60%	34.60%	12.24%
Debt:										
Total debt per capita	$748.55	$551.07	$462.48	$504.01	$430.78	$341.02	$515.95	$661.59	$516.86	$268.59
Interest per capita	$33.88	$32.65	$16.67	$22.91	$22.36	$15.10	$24.22	$27.24	$23.19	$14.30
Municipal capital spending per capita five-year average, 1971-75	$64.93	$102.37	$67.68	$72.42	$73.43	$49.88	$111.57	$120.09	$81.52	$46.75
Expense:										
Fire expenses per capita	$17.17	$28.48	$26.62	$27.75	$24.29	$26.89	$38.34	$46.50	$29.55	$10.32
Education expenses per capita	$237.58	$266.60	$212.36	$227.53	$249.22	$266.35	$240.03	$251.23	$236.94	$60.24
Health expenses per capita	$6.77	$7.37	$5.63	$3.57	$15.82	$7.67	$10.44	$14.33	$7.56	$9.07
Welfare expenses per capita	$3.57	$4.32	$1.84	$4.51	$12.52	$.60	$5.66	$24.58	$5.52	$14.81
Ratio of city full-time-equivalent employment to total local employment	2.40%	3.48%	3.28%	3.90%	2.73%	2.53%	5.93%	6.96%	3.98%	2.23%
Average city employee annual income	$8,206	$8,303	$6,694	$7,057	$7,587	$9,292	$8,342	$8,546	$7,746	$1,606
Current operating expenses per capita	$442.43	$495.05	$416.89	$469.79	$483.72	$486.93	$551.66	$618.21	$484.61	$120.27

Population (thousands) 1970	287.61	221.21	127.20	245.63	386.39	323.34	348.87	244.35	250.88	198.53
Population (thousands) 1975	323.45	208.34	131.88	248.38	411.11	310.28	324.91	221.82	248.86	190.75
Number of cities in cluster	6	6	15	14	3	6	11	5	—	—
	Hollywood	Kansas City	Port Arthur	Galveston	Denver	Omaha	Pasadena	Long Beach		
	Jacksonville	Stamford	West Palm Beach	Salt Lake City	Tempe	Grand Rapids	Springfield	New Haven		
	Bloomington	Decatur	Duluth	Albuquerque	Phoenix	Seattle	Louisville	Hartford		
	Irving	Madison	Mobile	New Orleans		Milwaukee	Dayton	Buffalo		
	Indianapolis	Rochester	San Angelo	Jackson		Daly City	Syracuse	Trenton		
	Baton Rouge	Fort Worth	Amarillo	Tucson		Evanston	Minneapolis			
			Little Rock	Tampa			Pittsburgh			
			Topeka	Spokane			Bridgeport			
			Greensboro	Austin			Baltimore			
			Montgomery	Atlanta			Boston			
			Eugene	St. Petersburg			Cambridge			
			Lincoln	Fresno						
			Wichita	Richmond						
			Pueblo	Savannah						
			Worcester							

Table 5.2
Variations in Social and Economic Conditions: The Statistical Means

	Small Dependent Population				Large Dependent Population				66 Cities Mean	Standard Deviation for All 66 Cities
	High Private Investment and Income	Above-Average Private Investment and Income	Average Private Investment and Income	Below-Average Private Investment and Income	High Private Investment and Income	Above-Average Private Investment and Income	Average Private Investment and Income	Below-Average Private Investment and Income		
Revenue:										
Ratio of local taxes to personal income	5.11%	5.65%	5.45%	4.48%	3.83%	5.40%	6.13%	6.43%	5.65%	2.26%
Local taxes per capita	$261.43	$311.74	$264.89	$206.67	$181.41	$277.11	$266.66	$273.49	$265.02	$106.41
Intergovernmental revenue as a percent of total local revenue	30.20%	32.20%	31.10%	33.30%	43.00%	35.20%	37.40%	37.50%	34.60%	12.24%
Debt:										
Total debt per capita	$690.32	$520.60	$491.32	$434.73	$475.70	$371.50	$478.90	$585.03	$516.86	$268.59
Interest per capita	$32.25	$29.42	$17.79	$20.03	$22.30	$18.34	$21.94	$25.49	$23.19	$14.30
Municipal capital spending per capita five-year average, 1971-75	$67.57	$99.09	$74.97	$71.23	$68.44	$53.16	$97.53	$89.87	$81.52	$46.75
Expense:										
Fire expenses per capita	$19.40	$30.79	$28.51	$25.36	$20.04	$24.58	$34.65	$35.30	$29.55	$10.32
Education expenses per capita	$254.22	$281.73	$231.53	$208.73	$196.79	$251.22	$216.60	$242.71	$236.94	$60.24
Health expenses per capita	$8.45	$8.63	$7.30	$3.85	$14.47	$6.41	$8.01	$7.31	$7.56	$9.07
Welfare expenses per capita	$5.40	$4.12	$1.77	—	$10.60	$.79	$5.15	$13.29	$5.52	$14.81
Ratio of city full-time-equivalent employment to total local employment	2.50%	3.75%	3.50%	3.07%	2.56%	2.27%	5.30%	5.28%	3.98%	2.23%
Average city employee annual income	$7,904	$9,103	$7,059	$7,658	$8,335	$8,492	$7,724	$7,375	$7,746	$1,606
Current operating expenses per capita	$466.74	$515.10	$464.89	$445.56	$419.29	$466.88	$482.93	$531.46	$484.61	$120.27

Population (thousands) 1970	230.20	221.24	151.11	258.60	636.71	323.31	290.86	240.55	250.88	198.53
Population (thousands) 1975	261.37	207.96	150.00	276.51	672.21	310.67	277.09	228.85	248.86	190.75
Number of cities in cluster	7	6	13	5	2	6	13	14	—	—
	Baton Rouge	Rochester	Amarillo	Tucson	Jacksonville	Decatur	Pasadena	New Orleans		
	Bloomington	Madison	Lincoln	Salt Lake City	Indianapolis	Evanston	Syracuse	Savannah		
	Irving	Seattle	Topeka	Long Beach		Omaha	Spring-field	Trenton		
	Phoenix	Daly City	Greensboro	Albuquerque		Milwaukee	Bridgeport	Atlanta		
	Hollywood	Stamford	Worcester	Austin		Grand Rapids	Boston	Galveston		
	Tempe	Fort Worth	Minneapolis			Kansas City	Montgomery	Buffalo		
	Denver		Eugene				Pittsburgh	Tampa		
			San Angelo				Louisville	Hartford		
			Cambridge				Dayton	Fresno		
			West Palm Beach				Pueblo	New Haven		
			Wichita				Mobile	Richmond		
			Little Rock				Baltimore	Jackson		
			Duluth				Port Arthur	Spokane		
								St. Petersburg		

Table 5.3
Tax Burdens under Different Economic, Social, and Structural Conditions

Social and Structural Conditions	High Private Investment and Income Cluster		Below-Average Private Investment and Income Cluster		Statistical Swing[a]	
	Ratio of Local Taxes to Personal Income	Local Taxes per Capita	Ratio of Local Taxes to Personal Income	Local Taxes per Capita	Ratio of Local Taxes to Personal Income	Local Taxes per Capita
Small dependent population	5.11%	$261.43	–	–	–	–
Large dependent population	–	–	6.43%	$273.49	+25.80%	+4.60%
Low population density	4.44%	$223.76	–	–	–	–
High population density	–	–	8.55%	$360.00	+92.60%	+60.90%

[a]Statistical swing provides a convenient statistical measure for quantifying the sensitivity of the Short List of Financial Variables to changing circumstances. In this table, statistical swing represents the percent of variation as social conditions shift from small to large dependent populations or population densities shift from low to high and as economic conditions shift from the best conditions (high private investment and income) to the worst conditions (below-average private investment and income). Statistical swing is also utilized to emphasize the percent of variation in municipal financial performance as economic conditions shift among the four economic clusters.

Intergovernmental Transfers

In order to analyze variations in transfers, we have utilized the same comparative technique as in the preceding section.[2] This technique is useful because it highlights the direction and magnitude of adjustment in municipal financial performance to differing economic, social, and structural conditions. The relevant data for intergovernmental transfers are contained in Table 5.4.

In principle, intergovernmental transfers are designed to reduce income disparities and alleviate social problems across municipalities with widely differing conditions (equalization). Historically, these transfers—whether from the Federal government to state and local governments or from state to local governments—have been largely targeted to projects to improve education, health, welfare, and other social functions. Among the hundreds of Federal grant-in-aid programs, few are directed specifically at stimulating economic growth.

The statistical swing data shown in Table 5.4 provide insight into two aspects of the sensitivity of these income transfers—as economic conditions change across the clusters (social and structural conditions held constant) or as social and structural conditions change (economic conditions held constant).

The former case reveals that as economic conditions worsen among cities with large dependent populations and high population density, the percent of intergovernmental revenue income does not increase. On the other hand, as

Table 5.4

Intergovernmental Transfers under Different Economic, Social, and Structural Conditions

Social and Structural conditions	High Private Investment and Income Cluster	Below-Average Private Investment and Income Cluster	Statistical Swing as Economic Conditions Worsen
Small dependent population	30.2%	33.3%	+10.3%
Large dependent population	43.0	37.5	−12.8
Low population density	30.4	35.9	+18.1
High population density	38.3	37.6	−1.8
Statistical swing as social and structural conditions worsen:			
Small to large dependent population	+42.4%	+12.6%	
Low to high population density	+26.0	+4.7	

economic conditions worsen among cities with small dependent populations and low population density, the percent of intergovernmental revenue increases. From the standpoint of addressing fiscal instability in cities, we find these swings to be counter-intuitive, inasmuch as the small dependent population and low population density cities probably face less financial demand than those with large dependent populations, high population density, and below-average private investment and income.

Furthermore, the most appreciable differences in transfer payments are associated with unfavorable social and structural conditions rather than adverse economic conditions. Note specifically that the high private investment and income cities with large dependent populations are getting considerably more Federal and state funds than cities with poor economic conditions. Indeed, the economically well-off cities with large dependent problems have the highest percent of intergovernmental revenue in the entire sample. This suggests that cities qualify incrementally for more Federal and state funds as social conditions worsen, irrespective of their economic conditions.

On the basis of this analysis, one may conclude that the intergovernmental transfer system seems to be far more responsive to worsening social and structural conditions than to changes in economic conditions. This may lead to fiscal difficulties in cities with large dependent populations that experience an economic downturn.

These conclusions were unanticipated and represent an important finding in this investigation. Analysis of individual cities within the four economic clusters will provide additional insight into this issue. Additionally, future research must be undertaken which analyzes the Federal and state components of intergovernmental transfers separately across a large sample of cities.

Debt and Municipal Capital Spending

It is important to understand the relationship of debt to municipal capital
spending as a feature of municipal finance. Higher debt often is, but should not
necessarily be, considered as adversely affecting the financial stability of a city.
When higher debt links directly into important public infrastructure investments,
private investment may increase accordingly, with economic growth the result.
This is the essence of municipal leveraging of private sector capital spending.

As the statistical swings among clusters in Table 5.5 show, the high private
investment and income, and small dependent population, low-population-density
cities have high debt levels, but do not necessarily have higher capital spending
levels. Note specifically that in every case, capital spending increases as
economic, social, and structural conditions worsen. In cities with large dependent populations and high population densities, the increase in municipal capital
spending is large and is accompanied by sharp jumps in debt. Conversely, as
economic conditions worsen for the cities in the small social and low-density
cities, the debt burden is, in fact, reduced. This may simply suggest that a
disproportionate number of cities with below-average private investment and
income are industrially aged cities which are beginning the costly process of
upgrading aging infrastructure.

At the same time, the lower debt ratio for cities with fewer social and
structural problems may reflect a basic conservative reaction to potential fiscal
stress, thus maintaining the balance between fiscal resources and service
demands.

Finally, it is important to note the disparity between the levels of total debt
and municipal capital spending across social and structural conditions. Again, it

Table 5.5
Debt and Municipal Capital Spending

Social and Structural Conditions	High Private Investment and Income Cluster		Below-Average Private Investment and Income Cluster		Statistical Swing	
	Total Debt per Capita	Municipal Capital Spending per Capita, Five-Year Average, 1971-75	Total Debt per Capita	Municipal Capital Spending per Capita, Five-Year Average, 1971-75	Total Debt per Capita	Municipal Capital Spending per Capita, Five-Year Average, 1971-75
Small dependent population	$690.32	$67.57	$434.73	$ 71.23	-37.0%	$5.4%
Large dependent population	475.70	68.44	585.03	89.87	+23.0	+31.3
Low population density	748.55	64.93	504.01	72.42	-32.7	+11.5
High population density	430.78	73.43	661.59	120.09	+53.6	+63.5

would appear that variations in population density have a greater impact on debt and capital spending than do variations in social conditions.

Current Operating Expenses
per Capita

In one real sense, the expenditure side of municipal fiscal performance is more important than the revenue side in the analysis of municipal financial performance, for there is a direct link between the municipal expenditures and service demands that stem from changes in economic, social, and structural conditions. Once the level of expenditure commitment is made in response to economic, social, and structural conditions, a balancing combination of tax, transfer, and debt financing must be brought about in order to balance the budget. In this sense, changes in economic, social, and structural conditions feed directly into expenditure demand, but indirectly into revenue-raising techniques. Changes in expenditure levels are also a relevant indicator of the extent to which a municipality attempts to fulfill the citizenry's demand for public goods and services.

Fire Expenses per Capita

Fire expenses per capita are an especially interesting analytical variable in that, as an operating expense, they track very closely the movement of other city expenses in aggregate, are consistently selected in factor analysis as a descriptive variable, and as such are statistically reliable across cities.

The variations in fire expenses per capita are clearly delineated as economic, social, and structural conditions change. Furthermore, there is an unmistakable pattern in all sixteen cases; namely, as economic conditions worsen, fire expenses rise. As expected, the higher absolute levels are found in those cities with either large dependent populations or high population densities. Overall, we believe that this variable shows the most logically consistent pattern among all the variables in the Short List. The relevant data for this cluster are shown in Table 5.6.

Education Expenses per Capita

Variations in education expenses follow an uneven pattern in response to changes in economic, social, and structural conditions. Larger expenditures on education by some cities reflect their relative affluence, while smaller expenditures by other cities may be largely attributable to historical underspending—for instance among Southern cities generally—on education. At this point in the

Table 5.6
Fire Expenses per Capita under Different Economic, Social, and
Structural Conditions

Social and Structural Conditions	High Private Investment and Income Cluster	Below-Average Private Investment and Income Cluster	Statistical Swing as Economic Conditions Worsen
Small dependent population	$19.40	—	—
Large dependent population	—	$35.30	+82.0%
Low population density	17.17	—	—
High population density	—	46.50	+170.8

analysis, however, we are interested in generalizing municipal financial patterns across the clusters as economic, social, and structural conditions change. Shown in Table 5.7 are percentage changes in education expenses as these conditions change.

Careful review of Table 5.7 shows a somewhat irregular pattern as economic conditions change, but a relatively consistent pattern as social and structural conditions vary. As economic conditions improve—that is, as there is a shift from the below-average to the average private investment and income cluster—there are noticeable and perverse changes in education expenses. In three of the four cases, education expenses actually decline as economic conditions improve. The shift to the next economic cluster shows an entirely different pattern. There are substantial increases in education expenses as economic conditions shift from the average to above-average private investment and income cluster. Note also the greater gains in education expenses in the small dependent population,

Table 5.7
Education Expenses per Capita under Different Economic, Social, and
Structural Conditions

Social and Structural Conditions	Statistical Swing		
	Below-Average to Average Private Investment and Income Cluster	Average to Above-Average Private Investment and Income Cluster	Above-Average to High Private Investment and Income Cluster
Small dependent population	+10.9%	+21.7%	−9.8%
Large dependent population	−10.6	+16.0	−21.7
Low population density	−6.7	+25.5	−10.9
High population density	−4.5	+11.0	−6.4

low-population-density cities. As the final shift in the economic cluster takes place to the high private investment and income category, education expenses fall off rather sharply. These patterns are seen graphically in Figure 5.1, pointing toward two generalizations:

The better-off cities (economically, socially, or structurally) spend more on education than their less well-off counterparts, although these higher spending rates do not follow an entirely consistent pattern.

As economic conditions shift beyond a certain point, education expenses begin to peak and then they subsequently decline.

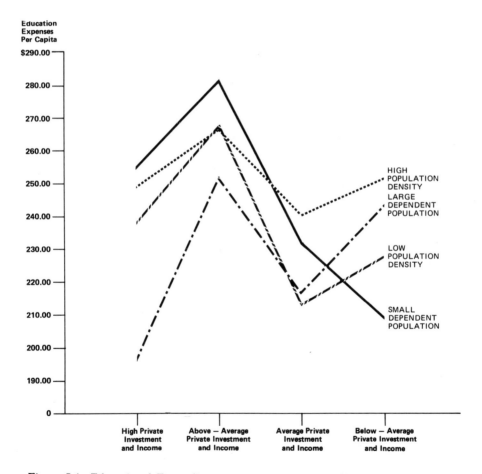

Figure 5.1. Educational Expenditures per Capita under Different Economic, Social, and Structural Conditions

The first generalization is certainly compatible with our *a priori* expectations, but the second is not. The latter may be the result of resistance to continuing expansion of locally funded education costs.

Health and Welfare Expenses per Capita

Before we examine the performance of health and welfare expenses across the 16 clusters of cities, two points should be made. First, it is generally argued that health expenditures are positively correlated with income and living conditions; that is, health expenditures rise as income and living conditions improve. Second, while welfare programs are usually managed at the municipal level, they are often subsidized, or completely financed, at higher levels of government. This is especially important to take into account because in this analysis we are interested in variations in gross health and welfare expenses irrespective of the funding source (to the extent that the data allow this segregation). This suggests that the variations across the clusters with respect to changing economic, social and structural conditions do not necessarily reflect the municipality's revenue-financing capacity.

Shown in Tables 5.8 and 5.9 are the levels of health and welfare expenses for cities with best and worst economic, social, and structural conditions. The statistical swings in per-capita health expenses shown in Table 5.8 are consistent with our expectations; namely, that health expenses are positively correlated with favorable economic conditions. Moreover, health expenses per capita increase with the presence of social and structural problems. Significant increases occur as structural conditions worsen, irrespective of changing economic conditions. Bear in mind that both Federal and state transfers are contained in these values and probably account for at least some of these shifts.

As expected, welfare expenditures, shown in Table 5.9, are significantly higher for cities with social and structural problems. Among cities with high

Table 5.8
Health Expenses per Capita under Different Economic, Social, and Structural Conditions

Social and Structural Conditions	High Private Investment and Income Cluster	Below-Average Private Investment and Income Cluster	Statistical Swing
Small dependent population	$ 8.45	$ 3.85	−54.4%
Large dependent population	14.47	7.31	−49.5
Low population density	6.77	3.57	−47.3
High population density	15.82	14.33	−9.4

Table 5.9
Welfare Expenses per Capita under Different Economic, Social, and Structural Conditions

Social and Structural Conditions	High Private Investment and Income Cluster	Below-Average Private Investment and Income Cluster	Statistical Swing
Small dependent population	$ 5.40	–	–
Large dependent population	10.60	$13.29	+25.4%
Low population density	3.57	4.51	+26.3
High population density	12.52	24.58	+96.3

private investment and income, welfare expenses per capita are two times greater for those with a large service-dependent population than for those with a small dependent population and almost four times as great for high-population-density cities as for low-population-density cities. Moreover, for the subgroup with below-average private investment and income, high-population-density cities have substantially higher welfare expenses than do low-population-density cities.

Ratio of City Full-Time-Equivalent Employment to Total Local Employment

Following the pattern of the foregoing analysis, the best-to-worst cases of differing social and structural conditions, along with the statistical swings, are shown for the ratio of city full-time-equivalent employment to total employment in Table 5.10. Once again, shifts in this ratio are of interest because they

Table 5.10
Employment Ratios under Different Economic, Social, and Structural Conditions

Social and Structural Conditions	High Private Investment and Income Cluster	Below-Average Private Investment and Income Cluster	Statistical Swing
Small dependent population	2.50%	3.07%	+22.80%
Large dependent population	2.56	5.28	+106.20
Low population density	2.40	3.90	+62.50
High population density	2.73	6.96	+154.90
Statistical swing:			
Small to large dependent population	+2.40%	+72.00%	
Low to high population density	+13.80	+78.50	

represent the relative size of municipal government. First, the ratio of municipal full-time-equivalent employment to total local employment increases as economic, social, and structural conditions worsen.

Second, the swings shown in Table 5.10 follow a most interesting pattern. Shifts within economic clusters in terms of social or structural conditions affect the size of municipal government at an inconsistent rate. Note that when structural conditions deteriorate under poor economic conditions, the size of municipal government advances to the highest level of all the subgroups, and at a much faster rate than as social conditions shift from small-to-large dependent populations. Note also that shifting structural conditions have a consistently stronger relationship with the level of municipal employment. This finding will be reinforced throughout these analyses—municipal government is larger among those cities whose economic and structural conditions are the least desirable.

Summary

At this point, it will be helpful to summarize our conclusions by stating that the linkages between economic, social, and structural conditions and municipal financial performance across all 16 clusters are uneven. In some cases, the linkages are of an irregular or inconsistent nature. In other cases, patterns are evident.

There appears to be a clear linkage between economic, social, and structural conditions and municipal financial performance in the following categories:

Ratio of local taxes to personal income (tax effort)

Local taxes per capita

Fire expenses per capita

Health expenses per capita

Ratio of city full-time-equivalent employment to total local employment

Furthermore, the variations for these categories follow a rather consistent pattern: when worsening economic conditions are coupled with large dependent populations or high population densities, per capita fire and health expenses as well as city full-time-equivalent employment will most certainly go up. This in time must, of necessity, be translated into higher taxes (as measured by tax effort and taxes per capita), which in turn may well set into motion a sequence of events toward higher expenses.

The real surprise on the revenue side is the role of intergovernmental transfers. As population density and dependent population increase, cities qualify incrementally for more Federal and state grant funds. However, as economic conditions worsen, there is little change in percentage of intergovernmental transfers. Indeed, for cities with poor social and structural conditions, the percentage swings in intergovernmental transfers from cities with best to worst economic conditions can be characterized as counter-intuitive. One can conclude that economic decline together with increasing population density and increasing dependent population can often result in fiscal stress. Under these conditions, locally derived financial resources are diminished and other resources, such as intergovernmental transfers, do not absorb the difference. Unquestionably, this insensitivity or inability of transfer programs to adjust to changing circumstances is one of the most significant findings of this research project.

In other cases, the impact of economic, social, and structural conditions on municipal financial performance was somewhat less clear. For instance, welfare expenses per capita followed an inconsistent pattern as economic conditions shifted but were sensitive (expenses rose) as shifts took place from small to large dependent populations and from low to high population density. The shifting education expenses, while following a generally consistent pattern across the changing social and structural conditions, all showed declines as economic conditions advanced from above-average to high private investment and income. This suggests that, as income and investment levels reached high levels, education expenses became less important in the municipal expenditure pattern.

The relationships are unclear when comparing total debt per capita with municipal capital spending per capita. Theoretically, there should be a close correspondence between municipal capital spending and municipal debt financing and private-sector needs. But this is not so. High private investment and income, low dependent population, low population density cities have higher total debt per capita, but they do not necessarily have higher municipal capital spending per capita.

Thus far, our analysis has dealt with the statistical means for the Short List Variables in terms of all 16 clusters. In the next chapter, we will examine the cities individually within each of the four economic clusters. As we move from the high private investment and income clusters to the above-average, average, and below-average private investment and income clusters, we will assess the relative importance of regional factors and the process of industrial aging in explaining differences in municipal financial performance.

Notes

1. It should be emphasized that this analysis is "cross-sectional," comparing cities at one point in time, not over a period of time.

2. Intergovernmental transfers in our analysis include both Federal and state grant-in-aid programs. Regrettably, data limitations prevented the statistical division between Federal and state transfers.

6

Analysis of the Linkages between Social, Structural, and Economic Conditions and Financial Performance among the 66 Cities

The next research step involves analysis of the financial performances of individual cities within the 16 clusters. In order to provide a manageable framework for the analysis, we will discuss the principal conclusions in terms of the four economic clusters: high, above-average, average, and below-average investment and income. This represents a departure from the analysis of the aggregate means in the preceding chapter. In that analysis, we examined variations in municipal financial performance with regard to their sensitivity to changing economic, social, and structural conditions across all 66 cities. This sensitivity analysis was accomplished through the systematic examination of the statistical swings for the Short List of Financial Performance Variables. In this chapter, we are emphasizing the shifts in social and structural conditions *within* each of the four economic clusters; that is, as economic conditions are held constant.

As we progress through the analyses of the four economic clusters we will be able to develop a more complete understanding of the linkages between changing economic conditions and municipal financial performance. Specifically, our analyses will show that the city's stage of industrialization must be given greater weight if these linkages are to be adequately understood.

Several important analytical refinements have been added at this research stage. First, we have included population size as an explanatory variable. The population sizes are listed at the bottoms of Tables 6.2A-D. The cities are arranged in each table beginning with the smallest and progressing to the largest, based on 1970 population size.

Second, the percentages of minority population and of pre-1939 housing stock appear separately in a number of tables. Although these are utilized as components of municipal social conditions in our analysis, we have singled them out because they are widely believed to be closely related to municipal financial performance.

Finally, we have provided information on the industry mix of the local economy. The industry mix information was derived from interviews with officials from the 66 cities. At this time, no attempt has been made to integrate this information into the methodological framework of this study.

High Private Investment and
Income Cities

Nine cities in the study have high private investment and income. Their major social and structural characteristics, as well as their industrial composition, are shown in Table 6.1.

Geographically, seven of the nine cities are located in the rapidly growing South and West. The remaining two are Midwestern cities whose economic circumstances differ sharply from those of their older, industrially mature regional counterparts. Bloomington is an affluent suburb of the Minneapolis-St. Paul urban area, while Indianapolis is an economically sound manufacturing city. It is interesting to note that both high private investment and income Midwestern cities experienced considerable structural change before 1975—the year for which most of our data were collected—which may well account for their presence in this cluster. Bloomington participates in the Minneapolis-St. Paul metropolitan tax base sharing arrangement; Indianapolis recently completed a major annexation program designed to bring suburban economic growth into the municipality's economic base.

All of the Southern and Western cities in the cluster have diversified economic bases and contain industries with national growth potential. The larger cities have grown to the point where there is widespread central-city agglomeration, characteristic of fully developed urban areas.

We may now turn to the variations in financial performance among high

Table 6.1
Social, Structural, and Industrial Characteristics of High-Income Cities

City	Region	Population Density		Dependent Population		Largest-Employing Industries
		High	Low	Large	Small	
Denver	W	●			●	Utility, beer, electronics
Phoenix	W	●			●	Electronics, finance, utility
Tempe	W	●			●	Electronics, manufacturing
Jacksonville	S		●	●		Shipping, services
Indianapolis	MW		●	●		Local government, automobile manufacturing, utility, chemicals, pharmaceuticals
Baton Rouge	S		●		●	Petrochemicals, finance, aluminum processing
Hollywood	S		●		●	Local government, tourism, finance
Bloomington	MW		●		●	Manufacturing, electronics
Irving	SW		●		●	Shipping, food processing machinery, electronics

private investment and income cities with differing social and structural conditions. The relevant data are shown in Tables 6.2A-D. Because of the overlapping nature and the small number of cities in this cluster, we have combined two of the subclusters—small dependent population and low population density cities—thereby creating three subclusters of cities for analytical purposes:

Small dependent population, low population density:

Bloomington

Irving

Hollywood

Baton Rouge

Large dependent population:

Jacksonville

Indianapolis

High population density:

Tempe

Denver

Phoenix

One may question the basis for classifying Tempe, Denver, and Phoenix as "high density" cities. This may seem misleading, but it results from the methodology utilized in disaggregating the cities into four economic clusters. Specifically, once the economic characteristics of the clusters of cities had been determined (the first statistical disaggregation), the cities were divided into two clusters—high density/low density—on the basis of the Z-scores within the individual economic cluster without consideration as to densities in other economic clusters.

Taxes

Among the most obvious characteristics of these cities are their relatively low taxes per capita and tax effort. Of the two cities in an older industrialized region—Bloomington and Indianapolis—one, Bloomington, does not fit into this pattern. Of the Sunbelt cities, however, the sole exception to the low tax pattern is Denver. It has been excluded from the mean ratios in the following tables

Table 6.2A
High Private Investment and Income Cities with Large Dependent Population

	Jacksonville	Indianapolis	Cluster Mean	66 Cities Mean
Revenue:				
Ratio of local taxes to personal income	3.57%	4.09	3.83	5.65
Local taxes per capita	$164.90	197.92	181.41	265.02
Intergovernmental revenue as a percent of total local revenue	38.20%	47.70	43.00	34.60
Debt:				
Total debt per capita	$554.41	396.99	475.70	516.86
Interest per capita	$25.82	18.77	22.30	23.19
Municipal capital spending per capita five-year average, 1971-75	$79.28	57.61	68.44	81.52
Expense:				
Fire expenses per capita	$22.77	17.31	20.04	29.55
Education expenses per capita	$245.91	147.66	196.79	236.94
Health expenses per capita	$11.67	17.26	14.47	7.56
Welfare expenses per capita	$6.77	14.43	10.60	5.52
Ratio of city full-time-equivalent employment to total local employment	3.17%	1.94	2.56	3.98
Average city employee annual income	$9,495	7,174	8,335	7,746
Current operating expenses per capita	$489.61	348.97	419.29	484.61
Population (thousands) 1970	528.86	744.57	636.71	250.88
Population (thousands) 1975	562.28	782.14	672.21	248.86

Table 6.2B
High Private Investment and Income Cities with Small Dependent Population

	Tempe	Bloomington	Irving	Hollywood	Baton Rouge	Denver	Phoenix	Cluster Mean	66 Cities Mean
Revenue:									
Ratio of local taxes to personal income	4.28%	5.01	4.09	3.58	6.32	7.92	4.60	5.11	5.65
Local taxes per capita	$180.88	289.41	209.10	216.72	264.49	442.14	227.30	261.43	265.02
Intergovernmental revenue as a percent of total local revenue	40.10%	27.10	5.00	33.30	31.10	32.90	41.80	30.20	34.60
Debt:									
Total debt per capita	$342.93	1,026.16	927.49	531.78	1,054.47	595.13	354.27	690.32	516.86
Interest per capita	$22.12	47.68	29.52	27.95	53.53	27.01	17.96	32.25	23.19
Municipal capital spending per capita five-year average, 1971-75	$69.08	57.33	80.49	37.58	77.29	84.11	67.11	67.57	81.52
Expense:									
Fire expenses per capita	$15.62	9.48	14.75	21.06	17.67	38.58	18.67	19.40	29.55
Education expenses per capita	$208.11	379.21	196.62	221.71	234.35	275.88	263.68	254.22	236.94
Health expenses per capita	$0.00	2.85	1.73	.59	6.54	47.11	.36	8.45	7.56
Welfare expenses per capita	$0.00	0.00	0.00	0.00	.20	37.21	.36	5.40	5.52
Ratio of city full-time-equivalent employment to total local employment	1.61%	0.95	1.40	2.85	4.10	4.18	2.39	2.50	3.98
Average city employee annual income	$6,422	10,892	7,027	7,428	7,221	9,622	6,717	7,904	7,746
Current operating expenses per capita	$358.94	564.15	340.08	437.66	474.11	515.16	477.06	466.74	484.61
Population (thousands) 1970	62.88	81.95	97.28	107.01	165.97	514.68	581.60	230.20	250.88
Population (thousands) 1975	84.07	79.21	103.70	119.00	294.39	484.53	664.72	261.37	248.86

Table 6.2C
High Private Investment and Income Cities with High Population Density

	Tempe	Denver	Phoenix	Cluster Mean	66 Cities Mean
Revenue:					
Ratio of local taxes to personal income	4.28%	7.92	4.60	5.60	5.65
Local taxes per capita	$180.88	442.14	227.30	283.44	265.02
Intergovernmental revenue as a percent of total local revenue	40.10%	32.90	41.80	38.30	34.60
Debt:					
Total debt per capita	$342.93	595.13	354.27	430.78	516.86
Interest per capita	$22.12	27.01	17.96	22.36	23.19
Municipal capital spending per capita, five-year average, 1971-75	$69.08	84.11	67.11	73.43	81.52
Expense:					
Fire expenses per capita	$15.62	38.58	18.67	24.29	29.55
Education expenses per capita	$208.11	275.88	263.68	249.22	236.94
Health expenses per capita	$0.00	47.11	.36	15.82	7.56
Welfare expenses per capita	$0.00	37.21	.36	12.52	5.52
Ratio of city full-time-equivalent employment to total local employment	1.61%	4.18	2.39	2.73	3.98
Average city employee annual income	$6,422	9,622	6,717	7,587	7,746
Current operating expenses per capita	$358.94	615.16	477.06	483.72	484.61
Population (thousands) 1970	62.88	514.68	581.60	386.39	250.88
Population (thousands) 1975	84.07	484.53	664.72	411.11	248.86

Table 6.2D
High Private Investment and Income Cities with Low Population Density

	Bloom-ington	Irving	Holly-wood	Baton Rouge	Jackson-ville	India-napolis	Cluster Mean	66 Cities Mean
Revenue:								
Ratio of local taxes to personal income	5.01%	4.09	3.58	6.32	3.57	4.09	4.44	5.65
Local taxes per capita	$289.41	209.10	216.72	264.49	164.90	197.92	223.76	265.02
Intergovernmental revenue as a percent of total local revenue	27.10%	5.00	33.30	31.10	38.20	47.70	30.40	34.60
Debt:								
Total debt per capita	$1,026.16	927.49	531.78	1,054.47	554.41	396.99	748.55	516.86
Interest per capita	$47.68	29.52	27.95	53.53	25.82	18.77	33.88	23.19
Municipal capital spending per capita five-year average, 1971-75	$57.33	80.49	37.58	77.29	79.28	57.61	64.93	81.52
Expense:								
Fire expenses per capita	$9.48	14.75	21.06	17.67	22.77	17.31	17.17	29.55
Education expenses per capita	$379.21	196.62	221.71	234.35	245.91	147.66	237.58	236.94
Health expenses per capita	$2.85	1.73	.59	6.54	11.67	17.26	6.77	7.56
Welfare expenses per capita	$0.00	0.00	0.00	.20	6.77	14.43	3.57	5.52
Ratio of city full-time-equivalent employment to total local employment	0.95%	1.40	2.85	4.10	3.17	1.94	2.40	3.98
Average city employee annual income	$10,892	7,027	7,428	7,221	9,495	7,174	8,206	7,746
Current operating expenses per capita	$564.15	340.08	437.66	474.11	489.61	348.97	442.43	484.61
Population (thousands) 1970	81.95	97.28	107.01	165.97	528.86	744.57	287.61	250.88
Population (thousands) 1975	79.21	103.70	119.00	294.39	562.28	782.14	323.45	248.86

because its tax and expense ratios are so far out of line with those of the other eight cities that inclusion would distort the comparative analysis of the statistical means. This suggests that Denver's municipal taxing, debt, and spending have outpaced the growth in its underlying economic resource base.

With Denver excluded, Table 6.3 shows only modest variations in taxes per capita across the three social/structural subgroups. Furthermore, all three are below the means for all 66 cities and substantially below the highest tax value for the sample. Note that the cities with large dependent populations have the lowest taxes per capita of the three subgroups in this cluster.

We have included the minority population ratio and the percentage of pre-1939 housing stock in this table. Note that all three subgroups are close to the 66 cities mean on percentage of pre-1939 housing. The large social ratio and high population density cities are close to the 66 cities mean on percentage of minority population. Both of these social conditions place pressures on municipal expenditures, but rapid economic growth has helped these cities to finance desired services while maintaining relatively low taxes.

Among these cities (again excluding Denver), there is no progressive increase in taxes as population increases. Indeed, when one compares (Table 6.4) taxes per capita for medium-sized and large cities (although there are too few cities to be considered statistically significant) one finds that taxes per capita are actually 15 percent *lower* in the large cities.[1]

Table 6.3
Tax Burdens within the High-Income Subgroups

	Local Taxes per Capita	Percent Minority Population	Percent pre-1939 Housing
Social and structural conditions:			
Small dependent population,			
low population density	$218.84	10.58%	73.66%
Large dependent population	181.41	21.29	83.55
High population density	204.09	20.52	72.45
Mean for 66 cities	265.02	22.20	80.29
Maximum value	556.36	52.20	96.40
Percent of 66 cities mean:			
Small dependent population,			
low population density	82.60	47.70	91.70
Large dependent population	68.50	95.90	104.10
High population density	77.00	92.40	90.20
Percent of maximum:			
Small dependent population,			
low population density	39.30	20.30	76.40
Large dependent population	32.60	40.80	86.70
High population density	36.70	39.30	75.20

Table 6.4
Relationship of Taxes to Social Conditions and Population Size

	Local Taxes per Capita	Percent Minority Population	Percent pre-1939 Housing
Medium-sized cities	$232.12	12.90%	74.99%
Large cities	$196.71	20.46%	77.23%
Percent difference between large and medium-sized cities	−15.26%	+58.60%	+2.99%

These findings run counter to a widely held assumption that greater population size implies higher municipal costs. Moreover, although the percentages of minority population and the pre-1939 housing stock increase as city size increases, for these high private investment and income cities such changes do not produce higher taxes per capita. Intergovernmental revenue, examined in the next section, may be helping these large cities hold down taxes by providing extra funds to cities with a large minority population and a high percentage of pre-1939 housing stock.

Intergovernmental Revenue

In Indianapolis, Phoenix, and Tempe, intergovernmental revenue as a percent of local revenue is very high. It is substantially lower for Bloomington and Irving. The remaining cities—Baton Rouge, Jacksonville, and Hollywood—fall in the middle. Again, we have excluded Denver from the analysis, although its intergovernmental revenue figure clearly falls in the middle range. The percentages shown in Table 6.5 remind us once again of the important conclusion generalized from the figures for all 16 clusters: intergovernmental transfer programs have become a significant portion of municipal operating revenue, but are most responsive to social problems (in this case seen as large minority populations).

Debt and Municipal Capital Spending

In order to evaluate the relationships among high debt, high municipal capital spending, and private manufacturing capital spending, we divided the eight cities into those with high debt per capita (Bloomington, Irving, and Baton Rouge), average (Hollywood and Jacksonville), and low (Phoenix, Tempe, and Indianapolis), and calculated the ratio of private to municipal capital spending. These ratios are shown in Table 6.6.

Table 6.5
Relationship of Intergovernmental Revenue to Social Conditions
and Population Size

Size Range	Intergovernmental Revenue as a Percent of Total Local Revenue	Percent Minority Population	Unemployment Rate
High	43.2%	19.96%	3.86%
Middle	34.2	20.15	3.86
Low	16.1	2.79	2.35
66 cities mean	34.6%	22.20%	4.43%
Maximum	64.0	52.20	8.30

Note that in the high debt cities, the levels of the municipal debt and capital spending are associated with higher private sector manufacturing capital spending. To a certain extent, a similar pattern exists among the low debt cities, although the ratio of private-to-municipal capital spending is only about one-half that of the high debt cities, but still slightly above the total sample mean. In contrast, among the average debt cities, the ratio of private to municipal capital spending is low.

Before we proceed, a comment is necessary on the significance of the ratio of private to municipal capital spending. This ratio, in all likelihood, reflects the extent to which city officials are leveraging private manufacturing capital spending; that is, using municipal capital spending in ways that improve the investment climate for business (for example, new or rebuilt infrastructure, such as wastewater treatment plants). Leveraging is increasingly believed to be an important technique for assuring the maximum local economic benefits from the

Table 6.6
Relationship of Debt to Capital Spending

	Total Debt per Capita	Municipal Capital Spending per Capita, Five-Year Average, 1971-75	Private Manufacturing Capital Spending per Capita, 1972	Ratio of Private to Municipal Capital Spending
High debt per capita	$1,002.71	$71.70	$243.27	3.393
Average debt per capita	543.10	58.42	55.52	.950
Low debt per capita	364.73	64.60	109.54	1.696
66 cities mean	$516.86	$81.52	$106.64	1.308

expenditure of public funds. When we examine the other economic clusters, we will observe substantial variations in the ratio of private to municipal capital spending—the leveraging effect—among the 66 cities.

Current Operating Expenses and Municipal Government

For high private investment and income cities the per capita fire expense is extremely low, as are expenditures for welfare. This reflects chiefly the higher level of affluence of the cities in this cluster. Education expenses, too, are not very high in comparison to those of other cities in the total sample. The highest for any of the 66 cities is $395.08 per capita. Among the high investment cities, only Bloomington, at $379.21, comes close to that level. It is also interesting to note that despite Denver's relatively high tax burden, it has a low education expense rate.

Finally, the municipal government size and average annual municipal employee income are interesting. Note that the ratio of city full-time-equivalent employment to total employment averages approximately one-half of the 66 cities mean and one-fifth the highest value. Municipal wages are roughly in line with the 66 cities mean. The low values for city full-time-equivalent employment ratio clearly suggest that these cities have relatively small but not necessarily high-salaried municipal governments. The figures are shown in Table 6.7.

Summary

Among these high private investment and income cities, low taxes coexist with low per capita expenses for fire protection and welfare. For high and average debt cities in this cluster (five of the eight analyzed), high municipal debt and capital expenditure appear to be closely related to high private manufacturing

Table 6.7
Municipal Government Size and Employee Income within the High-Income Subgroups

	Ratio of City Full-Time- Equivalent Employment to Total Local Employment	Average City Employee Annual Income
Small dependent population, low density	2.32%	$7,797
Large dependent population	2.56	8,335
High density	2.00	6,570
66 cities mean	3.98%	$7,746
Maximum	10.58	12,319

capital spending. However tentative, this is an important observation, because it seems to suggest that municipal capital spending can leverage private-sector capital spending; that is, municipal capital spending can be used to stimulate many times the same dollar amounts in private investment.

Above-Average Private Investment and Income Cities

Overall, 12 cities fall into this analytical category. The specific regional and industry-mix patterns are shown in Table 6.8, and the financial data in Tables 6.9A-D.

Table 6.8
Social, Structural, and Industrial Characteristics of Above-Average-Income Cities

City	Region	Population Density High	Population Density Low	Dependent Population Large	Dependent Population Small	Largest-Employing Industries
Daly City	W	●			●	Hospital, retail, public utilities
Seattle	W	●			●	Aircraft assembly, utilities, retail, paper products
Evanston	MW	●		●		University, hospitals, insurance
Grand Rapids	MW	●		●		Motor vehicles, manufactured equipment, instruments
Milwaukee	MW	●		●		Machinery and equipment manufacturing
Omaha	HP	●		●		Electronics, food processing, utilities
Decatur	MW		●	●		Machinery and equipment manufacturing
Kansas City	HP		●	●		Motor vehicles, airlines, retail, manufacturing
Stamford	NE		●		●	Business equipment manufacturing, corporate headquarters, electrical engineering
Madison	MW		●		●	Federal and local government, university, hospitals, food processing
Rochester	MW		●		●	Business equipment manufacturing, hospitals, electronics
Fort Worth	SW		●		●	Aircraft manufacturing, local government, retail

Table 6.9A

Above-Average Private Investment and Income Cities with Large Dependent Population

	Evanston	Decatur	Grand Rapids	Omaha	Kansas City	Milwaukee	Cluster Mean	66 Cities Mean
Revenue:								
Ratio of local taxes to personal income	6.47%	1.92	5.18	5.41	6.85	6.54	5.40	5.65
Local taxes per capita	$437.84	98.76	231.11	264.21	324.57	306.16	277.11	265.02
Intergovernmental revenue as a percent of total local revenue	18.70%	24.70	49.90	42.50	24.10	51.30	35.20	34.60
Debt:								
Total debt per capita	$374.13	187.14	271.60	374.91	697.64	323.55	371.50	516.86
Interest per capita	$15.33	14.63	12.32	18.30	36.41	13.02	18.34	23.19
Municipal capital spending per capita five-year average, 1971-75	$22.93	33.68	56.74	59.34	92.65	53.61	53.16	81.52
Expense:								
Fire expenses per capita	$22.93	18.30	27.03	23.77	26.91	28.54	24.58	29.55
Education expenses per capita	$314.39	248.02	287.33	185.22	199.77	272.58	251.22	236.94
Health expenses per capita	$11.15	0.00	.61	4.61	11.65	10.46	6.41	7.56
Welfare expenses per capita	$3.31	0.00	0.00	.26	1.16	0.00	.79	5.52
Ratio of city full-time-equivalent employment to total local employment	2.16%	1.18	2.46	1.84	2.68	3.29	2.27	3.98
Average city employee annual income	$9,404	7,682	8,946	7,814	7,412	9,693	8,492	7,746
Current operating expenses per capita	$548.46	348.85	514.32	379.95	501.61	508.08	466.88	484.61
Population (thousands) 1970	79.88	90.70	197.53	347.38	507.24	717.12	323.31	250.88
Population (thousands) 1975	76.67	89.60	187.95	371.46	472.53	665.80	310.67	248.86

Table 6.9B
Above-Average Private Investment and Income Cities with Small Dependent Population

	Rochester	Daly City	Stamford	Madison	Fort Worth	Seattle	Cluster Mean	66 Cities Mean
Revenue:								
Ratio of local taxes to personal income	4.90%	4.80	8.39	6.19	4.52	5.08	5.65	5.65
Local taxes per capita	$253.22	259.18	556.36	302.20	204.81	294.67	311.74	265.02
Intergovernmental revenue as a percent of total local revenue	34.60%	31.80	28.00	35.60	32.30	31.10	32.20	34.60
Debt:								
Total debt per capita	$332.91	229.44	1,095.64	518.35	474.75	472.49	520.60	516.86
Interest per capita	$14.87	9.86	89.69	18.63	21.67	21.78	29.42	23.19
Municipal capital spending per capita five-year average, 1971-75	$45.34	24.49	223.25	151.70	67.58	82.15	99.09	81.52
Expense:								
Fire expenses per capita	$25.44	20.51	38.68	39.02	22.53	38.57	30.79	29.55
Education expenses per capita	$322.71	298.73	318.86	312.33	197.89	239.85	281.73	236.94
Health expenses per capita	$0.00	0.00	21.74	5.55	5.26	19.21	8.63	7.56
Welfare expenses per capita	$0.00	0.00	15.81	8.92	0.00	0.00	4.12	5.52
Ratio of city full-time-equivalent employment to total local employment	2.44%	1.05	6.07	6.09	2.44	4.40	3.75	3.98
Average city employee annual income	$9,156	10,190	9,398	9,226	6,944	9,702	9,103	7,746
Current operating expenses per capita	$497.55	407.20	688.54	550.85	382.87	563.58	515.10	484.61
Population (thousands) 1970	53.77	67.25	108.85	173.24	393.46	530.89	221.24	250.88
Population (thousands) 1975	56.21	72.74	105.15	168.20	358.36	487.09	207.96	248.86

Table 6.9C

Above-Average Private Investment and Income Cities with High Population Density

	Daly City	Evanston	Grand Rapids	Omaha	Seattle	Milwaukee	Cluster Mean	66 Cities Mean
Revenue:								
Ratio of local taxes to personal income	4.80%	6.47	5.18	5.41	5.08	6.54	5.58	5.65
Local taxes per capita	$259.18	437.84	231.11	264.21	294.67	306.16	298.86	265.02
Intergovernmental revenue as a percent of total local revenue	31.80%	18.70	49.90	42.50	31.10	51.30	37.60	34.60
Debt:								
Total debt per capita	$229.44	374.13	271.60	374.91	472.49	323.55	341.02	516.86
Interest per capita	$9.86	15.33	12.32	18.30	21.78	13.02	15.10	23.19
Municipal capital spending per capita five-year average, 1971-75	$24.49	22.93	56.74	59.34	82.15	53.61	49.88	81.52
Expense:								
Fire expenses per capita	$20.51	22.93	27.03	23.77	38.57	28.54	26.89	29.55
Education expenses per capita	$298.73	314.39	287.33	185.22	239.85	272.58	266.35	236.94
Health expenses per capita	$0.00	11.15	.61	4.61	19.21	10.46	7.67	7.56
Welfare expenses per capita	$0.00	3.31	0.00	.26	0.00	0.00	.60	5.52
Ratio of city full-time-equivalent employment to total local employment	1.05%	2.16	2.46	1.84	4.40	3.29	2.53	3.98
Average city employee annual income	$10,190	9,404	8,946	7,814	9,702	9,693	9,292	7,746
Current operating expenses per capita	$407.20	548.46	514.32	379.95	563.58	508.08	486.93	484.61
Population (thousands) 1970	67.25	79.88	197.53	347.38	530.89	717.12	323.34	250.88
Population (thousands) 1975	72.74	76.67	187.95	371.46	487.09	665.80	310.28	248.86

Table 6.9D
Above-Average Private Investment and Income Cities with Low Population Density

	Rochester	Decatur	Stamford	Madison	Fort Worth	Kansas City	Cluster Mean	66 Cities Mean
Revenue:								
Ratio of local taxes to personal income	4.90%	1.92	8.39	6.19	4.52	6.85	5.46	5.65
Local taxes per capita	$253.22	98.76	556.36	302.20	204.81	324.57	289.99	265.02
Intergovernmental revenue as a percent of total local revenue	34.60%	24.70	28.00	35.60	32.30	24.10	29.90	34.60
Debt:								
Total debt per capita	$332.91	187.14	1,095.64	518.35	474.75	697.64	551.07	516.86
Interest per capita	$14.87	14.63	89.69	18.63	21.67	36.41	32.65	23.19
Municipal capital spending per capita five-year average, 1971-75	$45.34	33.68	223.25	151.70	67.58	92.65	102.37	81.52
Expense:								
Fire expenses per capita	$25.44	18.30	38.68	39.02	22.53	26.91	28.48	29.55
Education expenses per capita	$322.71	248.02	318.86	312.33	197.89	199.77	266.60	236.94
Health expenses per capita	$0.00	0.00	21.74	5.55	5.26	11.65	7.37	7.56
Welfare expenses per capital	$0.00	0.00	15.81	8.92	0.00	1.16	4.32	5.52
Ratio of city full-time-equivalent employment to total local employment	2.44%	1.18	6.07	6.09	2.44	2.68	3.48	3.98
Average city employee annual income	$9,156	7,682	9,398	9,226	6,944	7,412	8,303	7,746
Current operating expenses per capita	$497.55	348.85	688.54	550.85	382.87	501.61	495.05	484.61
Population (thousands) 1970	53.77	90.70	108.85	173.24	393.46	507.24	221.21	250.88
Population (thousands) 1975	56.21	89.60	105.15	168.20	358.36	472.53	208.34	248.86

Geographically, these cities are concentrated in the Midwest and the High Plains states, and to a lesser extent in the Southwest and West. Only one city—Stamford—is in the economically mature Northeast, and its recent growth pattern has been quite atypical for the region. Despite generally lagging economic performance in the Midwest, the cities in this cluster have been able to cut successfully against the grain of slower economic growth. Most of the cities in the cluster have a balanced manufacturing-nonmanufacturing economic base. The two most obvious exceptions in the entire cluster are Seattle, where defense contracting is the major industry, and Stamford, where the spillover of corporate headquarters from New York City has been the dominant growth impetus.

Taxes

One of the most noticeable patterns among these 12 cities is the significant variation in tax effort and taxes per capita. It is true that Decatur, with taxes per capita of $98.76, is one of the lowest in the entire sample, while Stamford, with taxes per capita of $556.36, is the highest. However, with these cities excluded, it is especially interesting to note that there are no appreciable changes in taxes per capita as social and structural conditions shift from more to less favorable. This stability may be explained in part by the relative degree of consistency in the minority and housing conditions among the cluster cities. The relevant data, excluding Decatur and Stamford, are shown in Table 6.10.

Table 6.10
Tax Burdens within the Above-Average-Income Subgroups

	Local Taxes per Capita	Percent Minority Population	Percent pre-1939 Housing
Social and structural conditions:			
Small dependent population	$262.82	12.94%	76.74%
Large dependent population	312.78	16.79	90.80
Low population density	271.20	14.14	78.85
High population density	298.86	15.35	87.05
Mean for 66 cities	265.02	22.20	80.29
Maximum value	556.36	52.20	96.40
Percent of 66 cities mean:			
Small dependent population	99.17	58.29	95.58
Large dependent population	118.02	75.63	113.09
Low population density	102.33	63.69	98.21
High population density	112.80	69.15	108.40
Percent of maximum:			
Small dependent population	47.24	24.79	79.61
Large dependent population	56.22	32.16	94.19
Low population density	48.74	27.09	81.80
High population density	53.70	29.40	90.30

In the transition from high to above-average private investment and income cities, an upward shift in taxes per capita is clearly evident. Three social/structural categories in the above-average cluster are above the 66 cities mean, whereas in the high private investment and income cluster all are below the mean except Denver and Bloomington. There is another dimension to this shift to higher taxes: there are only slight differences in the minority and pre-1939 housing ratios among above-average private investment and income cities.

Intergovernmental Revenue

When the 12 cities are aggregated regionally, the resulting patterns, shown in Table 6.11, reveal regional differences in intergovernmental revenue. The percentage for the only Northeastern city—Stamford—is low, reflecting the generally favorable economic circumstances of this city. All the remaining figures—except those for the Midwest—are below the 66 cities mean of 34.6 percent. Although the differences are not substantial, the intergovernmental transfer system seems to be quite effective in providing less money to cities with sound economies, but here, in contrast to our general findings, inconsistent in responding to cities with social problems. The conclusion is substantiated when comparisons are made to the minority ratio and unemployment rate. These inconsistencies may reflect local attitudes toward government assistance. There has been a fundamental difference in Northern and Midwestern as compared with Southern and Western attitudes about utilizing Federal funds to support local programs. Over time, this Northern-Midwestern preference for seeking

Table 6.11
Regional Differences in Intergovernmental Revenue

Region	Intergovernmental Revenue as a Percent of Total Local Revenue	Percent Minority Population	Percent Unemployment Rate
Midwest	35.8%	10.42%	3.95%
High Plains	33.3	18.29	3.50
Southwest	32.3	28.33	3.80
West	31.5	16.48	6.45
Northeast	28.0	16.13	2.40
66 cities mean	34.6%	22.20%	4.43%
Maximum	64.0	52.20	8.30

Federal grant funds has probably produced greater skill in channeling funds to their cities. As the analysis progresses, there will be additional support for this conclusion.

Debt and Municipal Capital Spending

We have calculated the average debt and municipal capital spending for cities in this cluster not only by region, but by population size as well. In all cases, we have related these to private manufacturing capital spending per capita in order to gain insight into the potential effects of municipal leveraging. In Table 6.12 are the key mean figures for debt, capital spending, and ratio of capital spending to debt by city size and region. (Stamford is excluded from the calculations because, like Denver in the preceding section, it is so atypical of the other cities in the cluster.)

The relatively small number of sample cities in this cluster notwithstanding, it is interesting to note the lower municipal capital spending to debt ratios for the smaller cities in comparison with the larger ones. One explanation may be that the smaller cities do not adequately leverage their debt—that is, they have less municipal capital spending per incremental increase in debt than their larger counterparts. Alternatively, there may be more intergovernmental aid to larger cities for capital improvements.

Table 6.12
Debt, Capital Spending, and Ratios of Capital Spending to Debt by
City Size and Region

Region	Total Debt per Capita	Municipal Capital Spending per Capita, Five-Year Average, 1971-75	Ratio of Municipal Capital Spending to Municipal Debt	Private Manufacturing Capital Spending per Capita, 1972[a]	Ratio of Private to Municipal Capital Spending[a]
Cities with less than 100,000 population:					
Midwest	$298.06	$33.98	.114	$ 43.69	1.286
West	229.44	24.49	.107	–	–
Cities with 100,000 or more population:					
Midwest	$371.17	$87.35	.235	$92.68	1.061
West	472.49	82.15	.174	58.59	.713
Southwest	474.75	67.58	.142	81.84	1.211
High Plains	536.27	76.00	.142	111.60	1.468
66 cities mean	$516.86	$81.52	.158	$106.64	1.308

[a]Data are omitted for private manufacturing capital spending in Western cities. This is because data were unavailable for Daly City, the only Western city in this cluster with population under 100,000.

Table 6.13
Education Expenses per Capita in Current and Adjusted Dollars

	Rochester	Stamford	Fort Worth	Seattle	Madison
Current dollars	$322.71	$318.86	$197.89	$239.85	$312.33
Adjusted dollars	$313.31	$279.70	$217.46	$235.15	$294.65
66 cities mean: $236.94					
Percent difference from 66 cities mean:					
Current dollars	+36.20	+34.60	−16.50	+1.20	+31.80
Adjusted dollars	+32.20	+18.00	−9.20	−0.80	+24.40

Current Operating Expenses

Careful examination of the expense items for the above-average private investment and income cities with differing social and structural conditions reveals a
number of interesting patterns. Perhaps most obvious are the variations in
education expenses. To a large degree, these differences represent regional
cost-price variations in wages, in other purchased goods and services such as fuel
and food, and in property taxes. Historically, the existence of these variations
has been minimized, thus giving rise to the view that the quality of education
lagged significantly in the South as compared with the North, because the
nominal levels of education expenses in the South remained so much below
national as well as Northern levels. To a degree this was certainly the case, but
after more than a decade of major inflation, these regional cost-price differences
have become much more significant and must be fully acknowledged.

To demonstrate the statistical significance of this line of reasoning, we have
adjusted the educational expenditures for five cities in this cluster.[2] The results
are listed in Table 6.13. In terms of current (or unadjusted) figures, the average
difference (without respect to sign) from the sample mean is 24.0 percent. After
the regional price influences have been removed, this difference declines to 17.5
percent—a one-fourth reduction. The statistical adjustment—that is, taking into
account regional price differences—will undoubtedly become more important as
citizens are more sensitized to the impact of rising prices on the quantity of a
public good or service.

Municipal Employment

It is also interesting to note the statistical differences in the size of municipal
government—as measured in terms of city full-time-equivalent employment to

total local employment ratio—in the industrially maturing cities as compared with the young growing ones. These are aggregated and shown in Table 6.14, along with the relevant percentages of the 66 cities mean.

It is apparent that the size of municipal government increases sharply from the young to industrially maturing cities. However, while the increase from a municipal employment ratio from 2.84 to 3.84 is significant, it is important to keep the two values in perspective. The municipal employment ratio of the industrially maturing cities is 3.5 percent below the sample mean, while the ratio for the young growing cities is 28.6 percent below the mean—a statistical difference of 25.1 percentage points. As our analysis progresses to the average and below-average private investment and income clusters, the impact of industrial aging on municipal costs will become more pronounced.

Finally, it will prove useful to examine different expense patterns among cities that are experiencing generally similar economic forces. Consider the five cities which are geographically tied to the Great Lakes regional economy, and whose expense patterns are quite dissimilar. The magnitude of the expense differences among cities in this relatively small geographical area is well illustrated by the ratios of operating expenses to taxes. These are shown in Table 6.15, and are listed from the smallest to the largest by population size. No discernible pattern emerges in these ratios when they are compared to the overall ratios for all 66 cities.

We have singled out these five cities, which participate in a relatively homogeneous regional economy, as examples of the difficulty of identifying clear patterns of municipal financial performance relative to changing economic, social, or structural conditions. It is important to remember, however, that we

Table 6.14
Differences in the Size of Municipal Government in Industrially Maturing and Young Cities

	Ratio of City Full-Time-Equivalent Employment to Total Local Employment
Industrially maturing cities[a]	3.84%
Young cities	2.84
66 cities mean	3.98
Percent of 66 cities mean:	
Industrially maturing cities	96.50%
Young cities	71.40

[a]The definitions of young and industrially maturing cities may be found on page 60. Of the cities in this cluster, only Seattle and Milwaukee belong to the maturing category; the rest are categorized as young cities.

Table 6.15
Expense Patterns of Selected Cities

	Evanston	Decatur	Madison	Grand Rapids	Milwaukee	66 Cities Mean
Local taxes per capita	$437.84	$ 98.76	$302.20	$231.11	$306.16	$265.02
Current operating expenses per capita	548.46	348.85	550.85	514.32	508.08	484.61
Ratio of current operating expenses per capita to local taxes per capita	1.253	3.532	1.823	2.226	1.660	1.829

are not attempting to explain the degree of intercorrelation across *all* economic and financial variables for the 66 cities. The discussion of the results from the correlation matrix of financial and economic measures in the preceding chapter reminds us that the relationships across undifferentiated sets of data are weak. The only way one can separate the influence of economic conditions and their effects on financial performance is to disaggregate the data base into logical clusters.

Summary

The cities in this cluster have higher taxes per capita than those in the high private investment and income cluster, and surprisingly, all of the four social and structural categories are above the 66 cities mean. The expense ratios vary substantially. Again, we are reminded of the complexity of the impact of economic, social, and structural factors on municipal financial performance.

Two final comments are in order. The first concerns intergovernmental revenue. In this economic cluster, the intergovernmental revenue transfer ratio seems to function somewhat independently of the social realities in these economically sound cities. The second comment relates to municipal debt, municipal capital spending, and private manufacturing capital spending. The cities in this economic cluster have lower ratios of private to municipal capital spending than cities in the high private investment and income economic cluster. Additional research must be undertaken before we are able to develop some kind of generalized explanation linking municipal debt and capital spending with private manufacturing capital spending.

Average Private Investment and Income Cities

In this economic cluster there are 26 cities. The specific social and structural characteristics are described in Table 6.16, and financial data are given in Tables 6.17A-D. This cluster contains a larger number of cities, thus permitting a wider

Table 6.16

Social, Structural, and Industrial Characteristics of Average-Income Cities

City	Region	Population Density		Dependent Population		Largest-Employing Industries
		High	*Low*	*Large*	*Small*	
Cambridge	NE	●			●	University, electronics
Minneapolis	MW	●			●	Manufacturing and food processing, data processing
Boston	NE	●		●		University, electronics, retail food
Bridgeport	NE	●		●		Machinery and electrical manufacturing
Pittsburgh	NE	●		●		Heavy industry, university, government
Springfield	NE	●		●		Insurance, manufacturing
Syracuse	NE	●		●		Motor vehicles, electronics, chemicals
Baltimore	S	●		●		Ship construction, utility, appliance manufacturing, railroad
Louisville	S	●		●		Electronics, auto assembly, university
Dayton	MW	●		●		Retail products manufacturing, utility
Pasadena	W	●		●		Electronics, university, business equipment, manufacturing
Mobile	S		●	●		Local government, paper products, water shipping
Montgomery	S		●	●		Local government, manufacturing, hospital
Port Arthur	S		●	●		Petrochemicals, shipyard
Pueblo	W		●	●		Mining, hospital
Worcester	NE		●		●	Machinery manufacturing, related industries
Greensboro	S		●		●	Textiles and apparel, utility
Little Rock	S		●		●	Aluminum products, electronics, diversified manufacturing
West Palm Beach	S		●		●	Machinery, equipment manufacturing, utility
Duluth	MW		●		●	Hospital, university, utility, railroad
Lincoln	HP		●		●	University, auto tires and related products, utilities
Wichita	HP		●		●	Aircraft manufacturing, food processing, electronics

Table 6.16 continued

City	Region	Population Density		Dependent Population		Largest-Employing Industries
		High	*Low*	*Large*	*Small*	
Topeka	HP		●		●	Federal and local government, auto tire manufacturing, railroad
Amarillo	SW		●		●	Food processing, apparel, railroad
San Angelo	SW		●		●	Federal government, electronics, university, apparel
Eugene	W		●		●	University, wood products, railroad, Federal government

range of comparative analyses. It also reflects considerable geographic diversity. Moreover, cities that are just beginning their process of industrial growth are juxtaposed with cities that have already passed into the mature phase of industrialization.

The key point here is that as the economic base growth slows and the stage of industrial maturity is reached, there will almost certainly be a period of fundamental disequilibrium between economic conditions and municipal financial performance. This disequilibrium results because while the economic base is either growing more slowly or stagnating, municipal expenditure patterns and practices, which have been established over decades, continue unabated. Furthermore, economic stagnation will be accompanied by an increase in the demands of the unemployed, welfare, and other service-dependent population groups that are left behind.

Planned financial adjustment is necessary to restore a more manageable and stable equilibrium between economic conditions and municipal financial performance. Admittedly, this adjustment process is beyond the immediate scope of this section; yet it is highly relevant to our overall analysis. We shall return to this issue in a subsequent chapter when we discuss in detail the limits of municipal financial performance.

The regional mix of the 26 cities in the average investment cluster is shown in Table 6.18. In addition to the regional diversity there is a wide range of industry mix, coupling cities that are large, agglomerated, and relatively isolated with cities whose economies are closely linked to nearby contiguous cities.

Taxes and Current Operating Expenses

We have emphasized before that the stage of industrialization is a significant differentiator among cities, and that it must be taken into account in the linkage

Table 6.17A
Average Private Investment and Income Cities with Large Dependent Population

	Port Arthur	Pueblo	Pasadena	Montgomery	Bridgeport	Springfield	Mobile	Syracuse	Dayton	Louisville	Pittsburgh	Boston	Baltimore	Cluster Mean	66 Cities Mean
Revenue:															
Ratio of local taxes to personal income	4.47%	4.76	5.90	3.09	7.09	7.18	3.45	4.48	9.18	5.30	5.13	12.42	7.22	6.13	5.65
Local taxes per capita	$172.25	199.76	363.44	131.50	313.63	297.54	144.56	184.65	375.39	227.86	227.07	516.31	312.65	266.66	265.02
Intergovernmental revenue as a percent of total local revenue	19.00%	37.30	25.50	29.40	33.80	54.30	17.50	58.00	30.90	40.90	41.60	33.90	64.00	37.40	34.60
Debt:															
Total debt per capita	$206.68	433.64	240.94	400.27	478.43	333.85	604.36	423.44	464.48	767.64	502.79	815.66	553.50	478.90	516.86
Interest per capita	$9.67	23.77	15.16	11.40	16.05	8.74	23.20	29.34	25.63	34.46	21.17	43.23	23.34	21.94	23.19
Municipal capital spending per capita five-year average, 1971-75	$35.17	64.55	54.54	66.84	119.37	154.00	49.14	154.47	51.78	106.26	41.59	156.12	213.98	97.53	81.52
Expense:															
Fire expenses per capita	$22.91	20.68	30.91	27.87	55.06	34.91	28.41	45.67	33.48	30.48	28.20	52.47	39.40	34.65	29.55
Education expenses per capita	$120.45	211.80	316.48	157.40	190.35	258.89	142.59	223.75	292.48	176.63	201.82	255.72	267.59	216.60	236.94
Health expenses per capita	$3.25	5.87	20.81	2.54	7.37	4.81	3.73	0.00	10.57	4.02	.36	14.09	26.82	8.01	7.56
Welfare expenses per capita	$0.00	0.00	1.11	5.60	5.38	3.78	0.00	0.00	1.99	0.00	.06	2.73	46.25	5.15	5.52
Ratio of city full-time-equivalent employment to total local employment	2.85%	2.16	3.54	4.12	6.68	8.44	3.32	7.32	2.98	4.11	3.65	9.19	10.58	5.30	3.98
Average city employee annual income	$6.748	8.537	10.017	5.273	9.602	7.292	5.667	6.883	10.419	5.267	8.217	7.785	8.701	7.724	7.746
Current operating expenses per capita	$270.40	378.75	650.88	339.86	477.64	492.80	334.97	496.95	659.75	449.09	438.86	774.01	514.18	482.93	484.61
Population (thousands) 1970	57.38	97.45	113.25	133.47	156.55	163.89	189.99	197.27	243.46	361.45	520.17	641.05	905.76	290.86	250.88
Population (thousands) 1975	53.56	105.31	108.22	153.34	142.96	170.79	196.44	182.54	205.99	335.95	458.65	636.72	851.70	277.09	248.86

Table 6-17B
Average Private Investment and Income Cities with Small Dependent Population

	West Palm Beach	San Angelo	Eugene	Cam- bridge	Duluth	Topeka	Ama- rillo	Little Rock	Greens- boro	Lincoln	Wor- cester	Wichita	Minnea- polis	Cluster Mean	66 Cities Mean
Revenue:															
Ratio of local taxes to personal income	4.78%	3.52	6.18	9.14	4.24	4.36	3.92	4.00	3.55	5.05	11.95	4.27	5.94	5.45	5.65
Local taxes per capita	$276.36	141.74	289.10	482.61	189.32	219.98	185.72	187.46	178.24	245.26	530.02	211.46	306.31	264.89	265.02
Intergovernmental revenue as a percent of total local revenue	44.00%	20.10	30.70	15.90	48.30	28.80	14.50	44.50	37.60	20.80	25.90	33.60	39.40	31.10	34.60
Debt:															
Total debt per capita	$274.75	219.93	1,086.76	396.36	714.65	384.59	284.92	312.00	311.61	501.76	371.44	829.91	698.41	491.32	516.86
Interest per capita	$11.08	9.23	22.03	23.56	28.48	16.38	10.96	15.43	11.92	8.47	12.85	35.15	25.69	17.79	23.19
Municipal capital spending per capita five-year average, 1971-75	$57.23	20.55	48.89	99.29	132.01	36.69	25.36	40.32	88.74	68.85	129.99	150.90	75.84	74.97	81.52
Expense:															
Fire expenses per capita	$33.85	19.15	29.96	43.03	33.54	31.23	18.21	32.99	24.24	18.77	36.73	20.74	28.13	28.51	29.55
Education expenses per capita	$260.64	187.49	276.99	184.44	298.86	195.36	185.29	186.66	219.12	223.10	295.90	223.81	272.23	231.53	236.94
Health expenses per capita	$1.85	5.42	0.00	11.99	.29	27.62	3.80	2.59	0.00	5.96	12.43	9.03	13.98	7.30	7.56
Welfare expenses per capita	$0.00	2.27	.27	1.01	.11	0.00	0.00	.01	0.00	0.00	19.36	0.00	0.00	1.77	5.52
Ratio of city full-time- equivalent employment to total local employment	3.43%	2.39	3.51	6.14	4.06	2.29	2.54	2.39	2.62	3.17	8.02	2.39	2.58	3.50	3.98
Average city employee annual income	$7,232	5,316	8,892	7,529	5,077	6,861	6,183	5,799	6,806	7,691	7,777	6,548	10,052	7,059	7,746
Current operating expenses per capita	$489.30	317.01	485.26	532.44	627.59	429.60	321.51	374.22	438.59	380.39	605.77	460.13	581.71	464.89	484.61
Population (thousands) 1970	57.33	63.88	76.34	100.39	100.58	124.94	127.05	132.48	144.20	149.52	176.60	276.70	434.38	151.11	250.88
Population (thousands) 1975	61.47	66.10	92.45	102.42	94.97	119.20	138.74	141.14	155.85	163.11	171.57	264.90	378.11	150.00	248.86

Table 6.17C

Average Private Investment and Income Cities with High Population Density

	Cam-bridge	Pasa-dena	Bridge-port	Spring-field	Syra-cuse	Dayton	Louis-ville	Minnea-polis	Pitts-burgh	Boston	Balti-more	Cluster Mean	66 Cities Mean
Revenue:													
Ratio of local taxes to personal income	9.14%	5.90	7.09	7.18	4.48	9.18	5.30	5.94	5.13	12.42	7.22	7.18	5.65
Local taxes per capita	$482.61	363.44	313.63	297.54	184.65	375.39	227.86	306.31	227.07	516.31	312.65	327.95	265.02
Intergovernmental revenue as a percent of total local revenue	15.90%	25.50	33.80	54.30	58.00	30.90	40.90	39.40	41.60	33.90	64.00	39.80	34.60
Debt:													
Total debt per capita	$396.36	240.94	478.43	333.85	423.44	464.48	767.64	698.41	502.79	815.66	553.50	515.95	516.86
Interest per capita	$23.56	15.16	16.05	8.74	29.34	25.63	34.46	25.69	21.17	43.23	23.34	24.22	23.19
Municipal capital spending per capita five-year average, 1971-75	$99.29	54.54	119.37	154.00	154.47	51.78	106.26	75.84	41.59	156.12	213.98	111.57	81.52
Expense:													
Fire expenses per capita	$43.03	30.91	55.06	34.91	45.67	33.48	30.48	28.13	28.20	52.47	39.40	38.34	29.55
Education expenses per capita	$184.44	316.48	190.35	258.89	223.75	292.48	176.63	272.23	201.82	255.72	267.59	240.03	236.94
Health expenses per capita	$11.99	20.81	7.37	4.81	0.00	10.57	4.02	13.98	.36	14.09	26.82	10.44	7.56
Welfare expenses per capita	$1.01	1.11	5.38	3.78	0.00	1.99	0.00	0.00	.06	2.73	46.25	5.66	5.52
Ratio of city full-time-equivalent employment to total local employment	6.14%	3.54	6.68	8.44	7.32	2.98	4.11	2.58	3.65	9.19	10.58	5.93	3.98
Average city employee annual income	$7,529	10,017	9,602	7,292	6,883	10,419	5,267	10,052	8,217	7,785	8,701	8,342	7,746
Current operating expenses per capita	$532.44	650.88	477.64	492.80	496.95	659.75	449.09	581.71	438.86	774.01	514.18	551.66	484.61
Population (thousands) 1970	100.39	113.25	156.55	163.89	197.27	243.46	361.45	434.38	520.17	641.05	905.76	348.87	250.88
Population (thousands) 1975	102.42	108.22	142.96	170.79	182.54	205.99	335.95	378.11	458.65	636.72	851.70	324.91	248.86

Table 6.17D
Average Private Investment and Income Cities with Low Population Density

	West Palm Beach	Port Arthur	San Angelo	Eugene	Pueblo	Duluth	Topeka	Amarillo	Little Rock	Montgomery	Greensboro	Lincoln	Worcester	Mobile	Wichita	Cluster Mean	66 Cities Mean
Revenue:																	
Ratio of local taxes to personal income	4.78%	4.47	3.52	6.18	4.76	4.24	4.36	3.92	4.00	3.09	3.55	5.05	11.95	3.45	4.27	4.77	5.65
Local taxes per capita	$276.36	172.25	141.74	289.10	199.76	189.32	219.98	185.72	187.46	131.50	178.24	245.26	530.02	144.56	211.46	220.18	265.02
Intergovernmental revenue as a percent of total local revenue	44.00%	19.00	20.10	30.70	37.30	48.30	28.80	14.50	44.50	29.40	37.60	20.80	25.90	17.50	33.60	30.10	34.60
Debt:																	
Total debt per capita	$274.75	206.68	219.93	1,086.76	433.64	714.65	384.59	284.92	312.00	400.27	311.61	501.76	371.44	604.36	829.91	462.48	516.86
Interest per capita	$11.08	9.67	9.23	22.03	23.77	28.48	16.38	10.96	15.43	11.40	11.92	8.47	12.85	23.20	35.15	16.67	23.19
Municipal capital spending per capita five-year average, 1971-75	$57.23	35.17	20.55	48.89	64.55	132.01	36.69	25.36	40.32	66.84	88.74	68.85	129.99	49.14	150.90	67.68	81.52
Expense:																	
Fire expenses per capita	$33.85	22.91	19.15	29.96	20.68	33.54	31.23	18.21	32.99	27.87	24.24	18.77	36.73	28.41	20.74	26.62	29.55
Education expenses per capita	$260.64	120.45	187.49	276.99	211.80	298.86	195.36	185.29	186.66	157.40	219.12	223.10	295.90	142.59	223.81	212.36	236.94
Health expenses per capita	$1.85	3.25	5.42	0.00	5.87	.29	27.62	3.80	2.59	2.54	0.00	5.96	12.43	3.73	9.03	5.63	7.56
Welfare expenses per capita	$0.00	0.00	2.27	.27	0.00	.11	0.00	0.00	.01	5.60	0.00	0.00	19.36	0.00	0.00	1.84	5.52
Ratio of city full-time-equivalent employment to total local employment	3.43%	2.85	2.39	3.51	2.16	4.06	2.29	2.54	2.39	4.12	2.62	3.17	8.02	3.32	2.39	3.28	3.98
Average city employee annual income	$7,232	6,748	5,316	8,892	8,537	5,077	6,861	6,183	5,799	5,273	6,806	7,691	7,777	5,667	6,548	6,694	7,746
Current operating expenses per capita	$489.30	270.40	317.01	485.26	378.75	627.59	429.60	321.51	374.22	339.86	438.59	380.39	605.77	334.97	460.13	416.89	484.61
Population (thousands) 1970	57.33	57.38	63.88	76.34	97.45	100.58	124.94	127.05	132.48	133.47	144.20	149.52	176.60	189.99	276.70	127.20	250.88
Population (thousands) 1975	61.47	53.56	66.10	92.45	105.31	94.97	119.20	138.74	141.14	153.34	155.85	163.11	171.57	196.44	264.90	131.88	248.86

Table 6.18
Regional Distribution

Region	Number of Cities
Northeast	7
Midwest	3
High Plains	3
South	8
Southwest	2
West	3

between nonfinancial conditions and municipal financial performance. Since the average private investment and income cluster includes cities in distinctly different phases of economic growth, it will be helpful to distinguish the relative tax performance for the cities in different stages. The relevant statistical means are shown in Table 6.19.

A number of very interesting conclusions may be derived from the data contained in Table 6.19 comparing financial performance of cities in different industrial stages. Before we discuss these conclusions, however, several preliminary points should be made. Note that only one of the minority percentages is at sharp variance with the 66 cities mean (the standard deviation is 13.78), but there is great variation in the mean population densities. The population density for the old industrialized cities is more than three standard deviations from the 66 cities mean, whereas the maturing and young industrial growth cities' population densities are well within one standard deviation of the mean.

We have seen that higher population density among old industrialized cities is accompanied by higher taxes and expenses. It also means that nearby suburban private-sector investment does not spill over into the central city economic tax base.

We may now establish the important conclusions. First, among the old industrialized cities there is high municipal capital spending per capita, but a very low leveraging ratio when this is linked to private manufacturing capital spending. Indeed, the .778 ratio is considerably below the ratios for the high and above-average private investment and income cities in the two preceding economic clusters. For the industrially maturing and certainly the young growing cities, on the other hand, the leveraging ratio is more in line with already established findings. Furthermore, the leveraging ratio for the growing cities is, as expected, high.

Second, it is evident that tax effort, taxes per capita, and operating expenses per capita become much higher as industrial aging progresses. Note, too, how the ratio of expenses to taxes rises from young to maturing cities and then falls off dramatically for the old industrialized cities. This results largely from the sharp increase in taxes, not expenses. The relevant percentage changes are shown in Table 6.20

Table 6.19
Industrial Aging and Municipal Financial Performance

Stage of Industrialization	Ratio of Local Taxes to Personal Income	Local Taxes per Capita	Current Operating Expenses per Capita	Municipal Capital Spending per Capita, Five-Year Average, 1971-75	Private Manufacturing Capital Spending per Capita, 1972	Population Density	Percent Minority Population	Ratio of Expenses to Taxes	Ratio of Private to Municipal Capital Spending
Old industrialized: Bridgeport, Boston, Baltimore, Cambridge, and Worcester	9.56%	$431.04	$580.81	$143.75	$111.88	11,227	20.64%	1.347	.778
Industrially maturing: Springfield, Syracuse, Dayton, Louisville, Pittsburgh, Duluth, Minneapolis, Pasadena, and Mobile	5.64	257.35	525.84	91.07	112.08	5,622	19.18	2.043	1.231
Young, early phase of industrial growth: Montgomery, Pueblo, Amarillo, Lincoln, Topeka, Greensboro, Eugene, San Angelo, West Palm Beach, Wichita, Little Rock, and Port Arthur	4.33	203.24	390.39	58.67	117.69	2,577	22.06	1.921	2.006
66 cities mean	5.65%	$265.02	$484.61	$ 81.52	$106.64	4,869	22.20%	1.829	1.308

Table 6.20

Statistical Shift in Taxes and Current Operating Expenses Ratios for Cities at Different Stages of Growth

From young to maturing growth:	
Local taxes per capita	+26.6%
Current operating expenses per capita	+34.7
From maturing to old industrialized:	
Local taxes per capita	+67.5
Current operating expenses per capita	+10.4

To many observers of municipal financial performance, we suspect that these two conclusions may be somewhat surprising, especially the rise in taxes vis-à-vis expenses. One can hypothesize that the rise in taxes results from the long-term deterioration of the aggregate value of taxable property in the economic base as manufacturing firms leave the city. This process cannot continue for long without having an adverse impact on the private-sector investment environment.

One might justifiably ask why municipal capital spending is so high for the old industrialized cities. There are several possible explanations. Some portion of capital spending may in reality be current expenses or vice versa; costs of capital repair and maintenance of existing and outdated infrastructure may be high; or municipal capital spending may be in categories unrelated to private manufacturing capital spending.

In a subsequent chapter we will discuss what is implied by these findings; namely, the necessity of bringing taxes as well as expenses down to a more sustainable equilibrium with economic, social, and structural conditions in order to improve the private investment environment, as well as the need to utilize municipal capital spending to stimulate, or leverage, private capital spending.

Intergovernmental Revenue

Significant variations are observable in intergovernmental revenue as a percent of local revenue. Overall, the spread ranges from a low of 14 percent for Amarillo to a high of 64 percent for Baltimore. This may be explained in part by the unusual success of Baltimore in obtaining categorical Federal grants. In addition, certain formula factors in noncategorical Federal grant programs may favor Baltimore over Amarillo. The Baltimore experience does not hold true for all of the old industrialized cities in this cluster; instead, the mean percentage for these cities is lower than that for industrially maturing cities, as is evident in Table 6.21.

This is contrary to what we might have expected. It suggests that the intergovernmental transfer mechanisms are not fulfilling their objective of equalization among these cities. This finding needs additional investigation on a

Table 6.21
Relationship between Intergovernmental Revenue and Stage of Industrialization

Stage of Industrialization	Intergov-ernmental Revenue as a Percent of Total Local Revenue	Ratio of City Full-Time-Equivalent Employment to Total Local Employment	Population Density	Percent Minority Population
Old industrialized	34.7%	8.12%	11,227	20.64%
Industrially maturing	39.6	4.44	5,622	19.18
Young industrial growth	30.0	2.82	2,577	22.06
66 cities mean	34.6	3.98	4,869	22.20

specific program-by-program basis, but it is clear already that while industrial aging and higher taxes and expenses go together, industrial aging and higher intergovernmental revenue do not. We find this unanticipated relationship interesting, inasmuch as there is a strong need among the old industrialized cities to exploit all potential revenue sources, in order to take pressure off local taxes.

We also find it very interesting to note the sharp increases in the relative size of government as industrial aging takes place. Indeed, it seems clear that the cities least equipped financially are the ones with the larger shares of city full-time-equivalent employment.

Current Operating Expenses and
Population Size

The relatively large number of cities in this cluster allows us to compare expense rates by population size as social and structural conditions change. The relevant calculations are shown in Table 6.22.

The discontinuities in current operating expenses as city population size increases run counter to much of what is widely believed about municipal financial performance and city size. These discontinuities introduce a certain amount of uncertainty into the argument that cities must necessarily experience diseconomies of operation—and thus rapidly rising costs—as they get bigger Nonetheless, it is apparent that high population density cities have generally high expense rates relative to those in other social and structural categories. This reminds us of a conclusion frequently derived from our analysis—structural conditions seem to have a greater impact on municipal operating expenses than do social conditions.

These conclusions must also be related to the increase in expenses as industrial aging develops. As population size increases, expenses often rise.

Table 6.22

Relationship of Current Operating Expenses per Capita to Population Size and Social/Structural Conditions

Population Size	Current Operating Expenses per Capita			
	Small Dependent Population	Large Dependent Population	Low Population Density	High Population Density
Less than 100,000	$430.52	$324.57	$388.14	—
100,000-249,999	463.76	493.26	428.00	$551.74
250,000-499,999	520.92	449.09	460.13	515.40
500,000 and over	—	575.68	—	575.68
66 cities mean	$464.89	$482.93	$416.89	$551.66
	Percent of Change in Expenses as Population Increases			
From less than 100,000 to 100,000-249,999	+7.7%	+52.0%	+10.3%	—
From 100,000-249,999 to 250,000-499,999	+12.3	−8.9	+7.5	−6.6
From 250,000-499,999 to 500,000 and over	—	+28.2	—	+11.7

However, expenses also rise as the city moves from the young to old phases of industrialization. Thus, it may be concluded that a wide range of factors—population size, stage of industrial structure, size of dependent population, and population density—must all be considered when one is seeking to understand the financial performance of cities.

Summary

The most significant distinction in the analysis of cities with average private investment and income levels was the introduction of the concept of industrial aging. As shown in the preceding analysis, a city's stage in this process is an important discriminatory variable in explaining the linkage between economic conditions and municipal financial performance. This pass-through effect has a number of identifying characteristics.

First, as a city ages industrially, taxes rise much faster than expenses. This is somewhat surprising, because as expenses rise the pressure to tap into alternative revenue sources—especially Federal and state revenue—is intensified. The conclusion seems to be that the industrial aging of cities does not necessarily result in proportionately more intergovernmental revenue.

In addition, clear and striking evidence has been offered that provides support for a most disquieting conclusion: while municipal capital spending per capita is quite high among old industrialized cities, it has very little favorable impact on private manufacturing capital spending. This stands in sharp contrast to the situation in high and above-average private investment and income cities, where municipal capital spending exhibits a close, and presumably functional, relationship to private capital spending.

Finally, among the old industrialized cities, the ratio of city full-time-equivalent employment to total local employment is quite high—more than twice the 66 cities mean, and more than two standard deviations from it. Clearly, the existence of such large municipal governments pushes expenses upward and brings pressure on taxes.

Below-Average Private Investment and Income Cities

In the final cluster of 19 cities, listed in Table 6.24, the special problems of below-average growth and its impact on municipal financial performance are examined. Among the 19 cities, 4—Trenton, Buffalo, Hartford, and New Haven—are old industrialized cities, and 2 others—New Orleans and Spokane—are in the industrially maturing category. At the same time, there are 13 cities in this cluster which have not yet completely started—or are in the early stages of—rapid industrialization. This is true of such cities as Tucson, Albuquerque, Jackson, St. Petersburg, and Savannah. Thus, some cities have low private investment and income levels because they have not yet begun to grow rapidly. On the other hand, other cities have completed the first full cycle of economic growth and now are confronted with reduced, or even stagnating, investment levels. Because of the statistical technique by which cities were allocated into growth clusters (the Z-scores), both the old industrialized and the newly growing cities fall into the same cluster, in consequence of their generally compatible low relative investment and income levels.

The regional mix of the 19 cities with below-average private investment and income rates is shown below in Table 6.23. The specific social and structural classification for these cities, along with their industrial characteristics, is shown in Table 6.24. Financial data appear in Tables 6.25A-D.

Table 6.23
Regional Distribution

Region	Number of Cities
Northeast	4
Midwest	0
High Plains	0
South	7
Southwest	4
West	4

Table 6.24
Social, Structural, and Industrial Characteristics of Below-Average-Income Cities

City	Region	Population Density		Dependent Population		Largest-Employing Industries
		High	Low	Large	Small	
Long Beach	W	•			•	Aircraft manufacturing, naval shipyard, university (hospital)
Buffalo	NE	•		•		Motor vehicles, manufacturing, chemicals
Hartford	NE	•		•		Aircraft engine manufacturing, finance, government
New Haven	NE	•		•		Aircraft engine manufacturing, university, hospital
Trenton	NE	•		•		Motor vehicle products, appliance manufacturing
Atlanta	S		•	•		Commercial airlines, automobile assembly, retail distribution point
Jackson	S		•	•		Banking, food processing, utilities, retail
New Orleans	S		•	•		Shipyards, university (medical), utilities, retail
Richmond	S		•	•		Tobacco processing, retail, government, finance
Savannah	S		•	•		Aircraft (manufacturing/ assembly), paper and wood products, shipyard, machinery
St. Petersburg	S		•	•		Business equipment manufacturing, electronics, appliance manufacturing
Tampa	S		•	•		Local government, utility, electronics, appliance manufacturing
Galveston	SW		•	•		University (medical), insurance, local government
Fresno	W		•	•		Federal government, utilities, food processing
Spokane	W		•	•		Aluminum products, chemicals, railroad, utility, hospital
Albuquerque	SW		•		•	Chemicals, apparel, retail
Austin	SW		•		•	University, local, and Federal government
Tucson	SW		•		•	University, Federal government, research, electronics (of business machines)
Salt Lake City	W		•		•	Minerals mining and processing, utilities, electronics, religion

Table 6.25A
Below-Average Private Investment and Income Cities with Large Dependent Population

	Galveston	Trenton	Savannah	New Haven	Jackson	Hartford	Fresno	Spokane	St. Petersburg	Richmond	Tampa	Buffalo	Atlanta	New Orleans	Cluster Mean	66 Cities Mean
Revenue:																
Ratio of local taxes to personal income	4.96%	8.71	4.62	9.57	3.91	13.42	6.98	3.73	2.78	8.12	4.41	5.96	7.26	5.54	6.43	5.65
Local taxes per capita	$210.84	333.64	179.03	406.38	176.38	536.45	295.24	167.60	137.23	402.30	192.18	234.27	334.19	223.10	273.49	265.02
Intergovernmental revenue as a percent of total local revenue	8.20%	45.30	33.50	24.40	47.10	39.00	30.00	49.20	30.70	43.80	46.60	59.70	26.30	40.60	37.50	34.60
Debt:																
Total debt per capita	$524.69	283.07	121.66	934.16	471.40	1,027.32	341.79	128.96	282.62	1,193.84	506.54	707.56	1,072.52	594.27	585.03	516.86
Interest per capita	$36.57	7.92	5.32	31.82	21.51	49.51	10.53	8.04	9.81	44.48	21.37	29.34	54.35	26.28	25.49	23.19
Municipal capital spending per capita five-year average, 1971-75	$44.09	49.05	37.11	141.21	79.65	191.30	73.19	60.07	43.16	108.45	59.22	152.04	160.21	59.43	89.87	81.52
Expense:																
Fire expenses per capita	$23.12	44.51	22.54	53.85	23.18	56.42	40.06	30.88	21.44	33.01	41.84	42.57	28.85	31.94	35.30	29.55
Education expenses per capita	$167.04	181.21	169.64	230.34	184.58	337.38	395.08	201.38	135.02	266.12	338.85	282.71	325.91	182.61	242.71	236.94
Health expenses per capita	$6.07	27.26	0.00	8.33	1.56	26.30	0.00	4.53	.01	14.64	0.00	.76	.04	12.85	7.31	7.56
Welfare expenses per capita	$.80	12.13	0.00	18.42	0.00	92.22	0.00	0.00	0.00	51.24	0.00	.14	3.50	7.60	13.29	5.52
Ratio of city full-time-equivalent employment to total local employment	3.93%	8.24	3.03	7.56	3.79	7.92	2.64	2.77	5.34	8.72	3.92	7.80	3.50	4.81	5.28	3.98
Average city employee annual income	$6,687	7,922	6,761	8,134	5,437	8,164	12,319	8,753	4,158	6,136	6,727	8,407	6,994	6,664	7,375	7,746
Current operating expenses per capita	$485.87	530.31	370.08	476.77	376.21	928.36	638.18	412.66	310.83	541.74	600.75	595.22	659.94	513.53	531.46	484.61
Population (thousands) 1970	61.81	104.58	118.34	137.72	153.97	158.02	165.97	170.52	216.07	249.62	277.74	462.78	497.02	593.47	240.55	250.88
Population (thousands) 1975	60.12	101.36	110.35	126.84	166.51	138.15	176.53	173.70	234.39	232.65	280.34	407.16	436.06	559.77	228.85	248.86

Table 6.25B
Below-Average Private Investment and Income Cities with Small Dependent Population

	Salt Lake City	Albu-querque	Austin	Tucson	Long Beach	Cluster Mean	66 Cities Mean
Revenue:							
Ratio of local taxes to personal income	5.37%	2.36	4.72	4.84	5.12	4.48	5.65
Local taxes per capita	$218.11	107.03	206.79	212.15	289.28	206.67	265.02
Intergovernmental revenue as a percent of total local revenue	23.10%	56.20	29.30	38.30	19.50	33.30	34.60
Debt:							
Total debt per capita	$124.59	390.96	657.12	645.15	355.82	434.73	516.86
Interest per capita	$5.46	21.90	28.17	26.98	17.63	20.03	23.19
Municipal capital spending per capita five-year average, 1971-75	$58.63	79.44	85.53	65.70	66.87	71.23	81.52
Expense:							
Fire expenses per capita	$21.72	26.47	19.03	24.43	35.14	25.36	29.55
Education expenses per capita	$185.81	237.70	189.35	206.26	224.51	208.73	236.94
Health expenses per capita	$0.00	4.22	5.74	.30	8.98	3.85	7.56
Welfare expenses per capita	$0.00	0.00	0.00	0.00	0.00	0.00	5.52
Ratio of city full-time-equivalent employment to total local employment	2.37%	2.91	4.07	2.74	3.26	3.07	3.98
Average city employee annual income	$7,016	6,599	7,147	7,422	10,104	7,658	7,746
Current operating expenses per capita	$331.86	457.48	410.73	467.31	560.41	445.56	484.61
Population (thousands) 1970	175.81	243.75	251.82	262.93	358.67	258.60	250.88
Population (thousands) 1975	169.92	279.40	301.15	296.46	335.60	276.51	248.86

Table 6.25C

Below-Average Private Investment and Income Cities with High Population Density

	Trenton	New Haven	Hartford	Long Beach	Buffalo	Cluster Mean	66 Cities Mean
Revenue:							
Ratio of local taxes to personal income	8.71%	9.57	13.42	5.12	5.96	8.55	5.65
Local taxes per capita	$333.64	406.38	536.45	289.28	234.27	360.00	265.02
Intergovernmental revenue as a percent of total local revenue	45.30%	24.40	39.00	19.50	59.70	37.60	34.60
Debt:							
Total debt per capita	$283.07	934.16	1,027.32	355.82	707.56	661.59	516.86
Interest per capita	$7.92	31.82	49.51	17.63	29.34	27.24	23.19
Municipal capital spending per capita five-year average, 1971-75	$49.05	141.21	191.30	66.87	152.04	120.09	81.52
Expense:							
Fire expenses per capita	$44.51	53.85	56.42	35.14	42.57	46.50	29.55
Education expenses per capita	$181.21	230.34	337.38	224.51	282.71	251.23	236.94
Health expenses per capita	$27.26	8.33	26.30	8.98	.76	14.33	7.56
Welfare expenses per capita	$12.13	18.42	92.22	0.00	.14	24.58	5.52
Ratio of city full-time-equivalent employment to total local employment	8.24%	7.56	7.92	3.26	7.80	6.96	3.98
Average city employee annual income	$7,922	8,134	8,164	10,104	8,407	8,546	7,746
Current operating expenses per capita	$530.31	476.77	928.36	560.41	595.22	618.21	484.61
Population (thousands) 1970	104.58	137.72	158.02	358.67	462.78	244.35	250.88
Population (thousands) 1975	101.36	126.84	138.15	335.60	407.16	221.82	248.86

Table 6.25D
Below-Average Private Investment and Income Cities with Low Population Density

	Galveston	Savannah	Jackson	Fresno	Spokane	Salt Lake City	St. Petersburg	Albuquerque	Richmond	Austin	Tucson	Tampa	Atlanta	New Orleans	Cluster Mean	66 Cities Mean
Revenue:																
Ratio of local taxes to personal income	4.96%	4.62	3.91	6.98	3.73	5.37	2.78	2.36	8.12	4.72	4.84	4.41	7.26	5.54	4.97	5.65
Local taxes per capita	$210.84	179.03	176.38	295.24	167.60	218.11	137.23	107.03	402.30	206.79	212.15	192.18	334.19	223.10	218.73	265.02
Intergovernmental revenue as a percent of total local revenue	8.20%	33.50	47.10	30.00	49.20	23.10	30.70	56.20	43.80	29.30	38.30	46.60	26.30	40.60	35.90	34.60
Debt:																
Total debt per capita	$524.69	121.66	471.40	341.79	128.96	124.59	282.62	390.96	1,193.84	657.12	645.15	506.54	1,072.52	594.27	504.01	516.86
Interest per capita	$36.57	5.32	21.51	10.53	8.04	5.46	9.81	21.90	44.48	28.17	26.98	21.37	54.35	26.28	22.91	23.19
Municipal capital spending per capita five-year average, 1971-75	$44.09	37.11	79.65	73.19	60.07	58.63	43.16	79.44	108.45	85.53	65.70	59.22	160.21	59.43	72.42	81.52
Expense:																
Fire expenses per capita	$23.12	22.54	23.18	40.06	30.88	21.72	21.44	26.47	33.01	19.03	24.43	41.84	28.85	31.94	27.75	29.55
Education expenses per capita	$167.04	169.64	184.58	395.08	201.38	185.81	135.02	237.70	266.12	189.35	206.26	338.85	325.91	182.61	227.53	236.94
Health expenses per capita	$6.07	0.00	1.56	0.00	4.53	0.00	.01	4.22	14.64	5.74	.30	0.00	.04	12.85	3.57	7.56
Welfare expenses per capita	$.80	0.00	0.00	0.00	0.00	0.00	0.00	0.00	51.24	0.00	0.00	0.00	3.50	7.60	4.51	5.52
Ratio of city full-time-equivalent employment to total local employment	3.93%	3.03	3.79	2.64	2.77	2.37	5.34	2.91	8.72	4.07	2.74	3.92	3.50	4.81	3.90	3.98
Average city employee annual income	$6,687	6,761	5,437	12,319	8,753	7,016	4,158	6,599	6,136	7,147	7,422	6,727	6,994	6,664	7,057	7,746
Current operating expenses per capita	$485.87	370.08	376.21	638.18	412.66	331.86	310.83	457.48	541.74	410.73	467.31	600.75	659.94	513.53	469.79	484.61
Population (thousands) 1970	61.81	118.34	153.97	165.97	170.52	175.81	216.07	243.75	249.62	251.82	262.93	277.74	497.02	593.47	245.63	250.88
Population (thousands) 1975	60.12	110.35	166.51	176.53	173.70	169.92	234.39	279.40	232.65	301.15	296.46	280.34	436.06	559.77	248.38	248.86

It should be kept in mind, therefore, that the private investment and income situation among these 19 cities does not necessarily mean that they are declining. It only tells us that relative to the other 47 cities in the total sample, these had the lowest rates of economic activity. Thus, the cluster is dominated by two rather distinct classes of cities: young cities in their early phase of industrial growth and old industrialized cities. Following the criteria established earlier, we disaggregated the cities into the appropriate growth stages.

Old industrialized (4 cities):

Trenton, Buffalo, Hartford, and New Haven

Industrially maturing (2 cities):

New Orleans and Spokane

Young, early phase of industrial growth (13 cities):

Tucson, Salt Lake City, Long Beach, Albuquerque, Austin, Savannah, Galveston, Tampa, Fresno, Jackson, St. Petersburg, Atlanta, and Richmond

*Municipal Financial Performance and
the Process of Industrial Aging*

The relevant statistical calculations for the 4 old industrialized cities and the 13 growing cities are shown in Table 6.26. To emphasize the differences between these two growth categories, we have omitted the one young city, Atlanta, from the subsequent analyses. Also, in order to assess more fully the impact of decline on municipal financial performance, we have included another cluster of cities: the high-growth cluster—that is, the 7 cities that are classified in the high private investment and income and small dependent population cluster. This will provide additional insight into the manner in which municipal financial performance adjusts to radically different economic conditions. A number of important conclusions may be derived from the data contained in Table 6.26.

First, note the steady upward progression in tax effort, taxes per capita, and current operating expenses throughout the process of industrial aging. Note, too, that the decline in the ratio of operating expenses to taxes is a result of a faster rise in taxes than in expenses. This point was discussed in detail in the section on average private investment and income cities.

The increase in the relative size of municipal government is also evident, especially when one contrasts the young cities cluster with the old industrialized

Table 6.26
Industrial Aging and Municipal Financial Performance

	Ratio of Local Taxes to Personal Income	Local Taxes per Capita	Current Operating Expenses	Ratio of Expenses to Taxes	Ratio of City Full-Time-Equivalent Employment to Total Local Employment	Intergovernmental Revenue as a Percent of Total Local Revenue	Municipal Capital Spending per Capita, Five-Year Average, 1971-75	Private Manufacturing Capital Spending per Capita, 1972	Ratio of Private to Municipal Capital Spending
Old industrialized	9.41%	$377.68	$632.66	1.675	7.88%	42.10%	$133.39	$ 77.54	.581
High growth[a]	5.11	261.43	466.74	1.785	2.50	30.20	67.57	141.87	2.100
Young, early phases of industrial growth	4.84	218.89	462.62	2.113	3.89	33.80	66.75	95.71	1.434
66 cities mean	5.65%	$265.02	$484.61	1.829	3.98%	34.60%	$ 81.52	$106.64	1.308

[a]This grouping consists of the seven cities with high private investment and income and small dependent populations: Tempe, Bloomington, Irving, Hollywood, Baton Rouge, Denver, and Phoenix. All seven cities are also classed as in the growing phase of economic development.

ones. Indeed, on the basis of these data, it appears that the size of the municipal government in industrially mature cities is about twice that in their younger counterparts. Unquestionably, this increase in municipal employment is reflected in the expense rate and thereby in taxes as well.

Intergovernmental revenue as a percent of local revenue shifts dramatically. In the analysis across all 16 clusters, we noted that a worsening in economic conditions does not necessarily produce higher intergovernmental revenues, although deteriorating social and structural conditions do. The percentages shown in this table seem to indicate that the intergovernmental revenue system more nearly fulfills its equalization function for these cities. Note that the percentages are highest for the old industrialized cities (presumably those with the greatest need), next highest for the young cities (the next in terms of need), and lowest for the high growth cities.

The ratio of private to municipal capital spending remains very low in the old industrialized cities as economic conditions shift from average to below-average private investment and income. The ratio for old industrialized cities in the below-average private investment and income cities is more than 70 percent below that for the high growth cities.

Finally, the ratio of private to municipal capital spending among the young industrial growth cities is also interesting, especially when compared to the same category of cities in the average private investment and income cluster. Growing cities in the below-average economic cluster have a much lower ratio than those in the average group. Again, this is consistent with our expectations, in that these cities have not yet begun, or have just begun, the process of industrialization. Note, specifically, that throughout the three stages shown in Table 6.26 municipal capital spending increases progressively, whereas private manufacturing capital spending increases from the first to the second and then declines in the third.

Summary

The analyses in this section suggest rather clearly that industrial aging should be taken into account in comparisons of municipal financial performance. Indeed, in future research, the stage of growth should be considered an integral component of the list of classificatory variables, along with level of private investment and income, social and structural conditions, and population size. Furthermore, the generally consistent sequence that financial variables pass through during this process of industrial aging is most interesting. Of particular significance are the sharp rise in taxes per capita, the increase in municipal employment, and the deterioration in the ratio of municipal capital spending to private capital spending. Taken together, this combination of factors adds up to an environment that is neither financially sound nor economically sustainable.

A final observation should be made about the municipal performance of Trenton. A careful examination shows that Trenton's tax, debt, and expense figures are in sharp contrast to those of the other old industrialized cities in this economic cluster—Buffalo, Hartford, and New Haven. This point will be elaborated in the next chapter, but it should not go unnoticed that at least some cities can buck the strong trend toward higher taxes, debt, and expenses that accompanies the process of industrial aging.

We may conclude this chapter by restating one of the major research goals of this book: to create a methodology for classifying cities according to their economic, social, and structural conditions and to establish the linkages between these conditions and municipal financial performance. At this point in the analysis, these research goals have been satisfied. In the next chapter, we will attempt to relate the analysis to the issue of municipal fiscal stress.

Notes

1. The medium-sized cities were Bloomington, Irving, Hollywood, Baton Rouge, and Tempe; the large cities were Jacksonville, Indianapolis, and Phoenix.

2. To make the statistical adjustment to remove the influence of regional prices on educational expenses, we used the U.S. Department of Labor Intermediate Standard of Living Budget for Autumn 1975. This statistical transformation adjusts the price relationships across the cities by removing the regional price differences. Thus, the adjusted dollar spending rates represent the levels of educational expenditures per capita as if there were no regional price differences.

7 The Limits of Municipal Expenses, Debt, and Taxes

Our findings underscore the need to move toward a more precise definition of municipal fiscal stress. Municipal fiscal stress is typically defined in terms of social, economic, and structural symptoms such as older housing stock, high poverty ratios, or population decline. In reality, municipal fiscal stress is much broader than a decline, or stagnation, in such variables. On the basis of this analysis, we believe that municipal fiscal stress should be described in terms of a dynamic adjustment process between financial capacity (the city's underlying economic resources) and demand (the citizenry's expressed need and desire for public goods and services).

Limits and Fiscal Stress

An imbalance between financial capacity and demand for public goods and services cannot be sustained for long without serious repercussions on the tax rate and debt servicing. Our analysis suggests that such an imbalance occurs for at least four reasons.

The first reason is the tendency for government to enact new programs and to expand existing ones without a complete assessment of the impact on current and future economic resources. The benefits from new programs can be concentrated, that is, targeted to voters who support a specific program. The costs of these programs, however, are diffused among all taxpayers. In the absence of a countervailing force to hold down costs, concentrating benefits while diffusing costs creates incentives for ever-increasing public goods and services.

The problems of fiscal imbalance posed by growth in government are compounded at the municipal level, where the demand for public goods and services is not generated by the same group of individuals (possibly not even city residents, in the case of commuters) who furnish the revenue to finance them. In fact, in all cities with narrowly defined geographic areas, the broader metropolitan structure actually works to reinforce this mismatch, allowing it to become more pronounced over time as the economic base of the central city erodes and suburban growth accelerates.

The second reason for this imbalance is the lack of political risk-reward incentives for guiding municipal management toward a consistent balance between revenue and expenses and the absence of performance evaluation tools which penalize cumulative operating deficits. Rather than striving for the ideal situation where marginal financial adjustments are made within an environment of cost-effective management, a municipality, even under the best conditions, tends to set total revenue equal to total expense. In the best of years, the municipality "breaks even." This problem is greatly compounded by the fact that spending and taxing levels are not always determined at the municipal level. The Federal grant-in-aid system has long been recognized as providing an attractive inducement to spend—perhaps on unnecessary or nonessential programs—by funding portions of local program costs, in some cases as much as 90 percent. Moreover, in recent years state governments have increasingly mandated new programs, leaving local government to provide the requisite funds.

The third reason for a fiscal imbalance in municipal government is inherent in the tax structure itself. Specifically, it lies in the overreliance on local property taxes. This problem can easily be appreciated by considering two sets of statistics. During the period 1960 to 1971, municipal expenditures rose at an average annual rate of 9.7 percent, compared with an average rise in GNP of 7.3 percent. Implied in these two rates of increase is a GNP elasticity in local expenditures of 1.33 percent; that is, for every $1.00 increase in GNP, municipal expenditures increase $1.33. On the other hand, municipal revenues—local property taxes (usually in excess of 50 percent of total municipal receipts)—user charges, and Federal or state transfers, unlike municipal expenditures, tend to increase on a one-to-one ratio with GNP. Thus, there is a constant pressure for municipalities to raise taxes to make ends meet.

Municipal expenditures have risen much faster than overall economic growth for several reasons: (1) municipal wages can rise without an accompanying increase (offset) in productivity; (2) greater urbanization—coupled with central city decline—increases the demand for services (fire, police, and others); and, (3) governmental delivery of public goods is essentially labor intensive. When this elasticity mismatch is combined with the mismatch in the counter-cyclical timing of the tax versus expense increases and the downward rigidity of municipal expenditure levels (especially with union-negotiated wage rates), the magnitude of this municipal fiscal dilemma is clear.

The final reason for the fiscal imbalance relates to the process of industrial aging. As the process of industrial aging advances, economic growth slows and maturity is reached. There will be a period in which there may well be a fundamental disequilibrium between economic, social, and structural conditions and municipal financial performance. This occurs because the economic base is either growing more slowly or stagnating, while municipal expenditure patterns and practices—which have been built up over decades—continue on their own dynamic momentum. Furthermore, accompanying the economic stagnation will be an increase in the demands of the unemployed, welfare recipients, and other service-dependent population groups that are left behind, thus bringing additional expense pressure directly on the municipality and resulting in increased revenue needs.

The growth in the cost of services *per se* is an important statistical indicator, but it must be related to the city's resources. Until the post-World War II era, local revenue (taxes, fees, and so on) rose in direct proportion to costs. More recently, state and Federal activities have either taken over functions once directly funded by the city or provided payments to the city in the form of grants that support specific activities or general revenue needs. In one sense, this has been viewed as positive (as for example in the case of higher educational expenses), but in another sense it has sown the seeds of excess (as in encouraging future commitments against municipal resources irrespective of underlying economic resource conditions).

As these resource requirements rise, more and more of a city's individual resource capacity must be absorbed. Fiscal stress arises as the result of the city's cumulatively exceeding resource limits. But even when these limits are exceeded, there still may be some "play in the line"; namely, marginal adjustments may be made to expand the expense barriers through additional transfers, attraction of new private investment, or improvements in managerial efficiency.

We may, therefore, conclude that there are barriers, or limits, to the amount of resources available to satisfy a city's service and social needs. At issue, generally, is the allocation of those resources among a myriad of highly competing needs, such as public safety, education, aid to the indigent, and general government services. The types and number of services are to some degree a reflection of the desires of the city's residents, of local operating costs within the geographic area, and of managerial discretion.

The concept of limits does not provide a definitive and unchanging barrier. Rather, it is a dynamic concept against which municipal tax, debt, and expense levels may be judged. As such, it provides a practical basis for comparing the relative financial performance among cities. It should be emphasized that limits can change over time, reflecting changes in taxpayer preferences and developments in the national economy.

For cities which have reached the stage of industrial maturity, achieving a balance between economic resources and municipal financial performance can be especially troublesome. Unless new sources of economic activity are forthcoming, the only way to solve the problem is through planned financial adjustment.

Planned financial adjustment is necessary to restore a more manageable and financially stable equilibrium between economic, social, and structural conditions and municipal financial performance. Admittedly, the specific steps that a city must undertake to bring about this adjustment process—implying a downward reduction in expenditure rates—are beyond the immediate scope of this study. Nonetheless, we believe that a comprehensive analysis of the sequence of steps into and out of this state of financial disequilibrium holds the key to a more complete understanding of municipal fiscal stress. Until new research is completed, we believe that the concept of limits will provide a workable definition for ongoing research. Municipal financial limits (stress) can only be defined in terms of the rate at which a city's tax, debt, and expense rates approach reasonable, or sustainable, outer boundaries relative to cities with generally comparable economic, social, and structural conditions.

With the conceptual framework of limits in mind, we may justifiably ask: how well have the 66 cities performed?

A Closer Examination of Limits: The Experience of the 66 U.S. Cities

As we shift our discussion from the conceptualization of municipal limits to its measurement, two important issues must be addressed. The first concerns the empirical delimitation of the outer boundaries, or limits: specifically, how meaningful taxing, debt, and spending limits can be determined statistically so that when a city has approached or exceeded them the result is fiscal stress. The second concerns the need to judge tax, debt, and expense rates in terms of underlying resource capacity. Certainly, no city with high expense rates *per se* should be considered stressed if it has the underlying economic capacity to fund high rates of spending. In this section we will analyze the performance of the 66 cities in terms of these two issues.

The most straightforward, although somewhat simplistic, approach to municipal limits is to compare statistically relative tax, debt, and spending rates across all 66 cities to the most extreme (the maximum values) for all the cities in the sample. Using this approach, we have prepared a table in which the tax, transfer, debt, and expense ratios for 11 selected cities are expressed as a percent of the maximum value for all 66 cities.

We selected these 11 cities because, among the total sample of 66 cities, their financial patterns have placed them in, or close to, the zone of the highest values for the overall sample. In other words, the numerical values listed under the column heading "Maximum Value for All 66 Cities" are simply the most extreme (the highest) value in each of the 13 revenue and expense Short List Variables. Overall, these maximum values are scattered throughout 6 individual cities in the total sample. We have also included four of the maximum values for social, structural, and economic variables in order to develop a more complete understanding of the connection between these conditions and municipal financial performance.

Interpretation of the ratios in Table 7.1 requires a brief explanation. Note, for instance, that Buffalo's tax effort is 44.4 percent of the maximum values for all 66 cities in the sample. The city with the highest tax effort is Hartford, and so its proportion is expressed as 1.00. Interpretation of the nonfinancial variables is the same. A number of interesting conclusions about the concept of limits may be derived from Table 7.1.

First, only four cities—Hartford, Stamford, Baltimore, and Fresno—contain financial ratios that are at the absolute maximums in more than one variable. Hartford reaches the limit in four variables, Stamford in three, Fresno in two,

Table 7.1
The Limits of Municipal Expense, Debt, and Tax

	Maximum Value for All 66 Cities	Ratio of Maximum Value										
		Buffalo	Denver	Stamford	Hartford	Pittsburgh	Boston	Richmond	Trenton	Atlanta	Baltimore	Fresno
Revenue:												
Ratio of local taxes to personal income	13.42%	.444	.590	.625	1.000	.382	.926	.605	.649	.541	.538	.520
Local taxes per capita	$556.36	.421	.795	1.000	.964	.408	.928	.723	.600	.601	.562	.531
Intergovernmental revenue as a percent of total local revenue	64.00%	.933	.514	.438	.609	.650	.530	.684	.708	.411	1.000	.469
Debt:												
Total debt per capita	$1,193.84	.593	.499	.918	.861	.421	.683	1.000	.237	.898	.464	.286
Interest per capita	$89.69	.327	.301	1.000	.552	.236	.482	.496	.088	.606	.260	.117
Municipal capital spending per capita five-year average, 1971-75	$223.25	.681	.377	1.000	.857	.186	.699	.844	.220	.717	.958	.328
Expense:												
Fire expenses per capita	$56.42	.755	.684	.686	1.000	.500	.930	.585	.789	.511	.698	.710
Education expenses per capita	$395.08	.716	.698	.807	.854	.511	.647	.674	.459	.824	.677	1.000
Health expenses per capita	$47.11	.016	1.000	.462	.558	.008	.299	.311	.579	.001	.569	.000
Welfare expenses per capita	$92.22	.001	.403	.171	1.000	.001	.030	.556	.132	.038	.502	.000
Ratio of city full-time-equivalent employment to total local employment	10.58%	.737	.395	.574	.749	.345	.869	.824	.779	.331	1.000	.250
Average city employee annual income	$12,319	.682	.781	.763	.663	.667	.632	.498	.643	.568	.706	1.000

Table 7.1 continued

	Maximum Value for All 66 Cities	Ratio of Maximum Value										
		Buffalo	Denver	Stamford	Hartford	Pittsburgh	Boston	Richmond	Trenton	Atlanta	Baltimore	Fresno
Current operating expenses per capita	$928.36	.641	.663	.742	1.000	.473	.833	.583	.571	.711	.554	.687
Social, structural, and economic variables:												
Percent minority population	52.20%	.405	.497	.309	.684	.389	.368	.815	.773	1.000	.906	.526
Percent pre-1939 housing	96.40%	1.000	.823	.844	.941	.971	.984	.884	.999	.895	.879	.746
Population density	16,187	.692	.334	.176	.561	.582	.861	.256	.863	.234	.715	.245
Manufacturing capital spending per capita	$569.38	.179	.154	.228	.082	.070	.102	.621	.188	.175	.254	.084

and Baltimore in two. This suggests rather clearly that no city in the total sample spends or taxes at high absolute rates in all variables. In part, this reflects the reality that different levels of government both supply revenue and undertake expenditures for any given city and offers support for the conclusion that "financial" leeway with respect to a city's own resources still exists. Admittedly, a growing number of states have enacted tighter restrictions on local taxing and spending authority. Thus, the absolute maximum limits in some categories may not actually be attainable for all cities. Nonetheless, the vast majority of cities in our data base are not affected substantially by controls on their local fiscal powers.

Second, it is interesting to note that there are relatively few cases in which actual financial perfomance ratios exceed 90 percent. This information is tabulated in Table 7.2. The table is differentiated in terms of whether the greater-than-90-percent rate occurred in a primary, or aggregate, spending or revenue performance measure or in one of the partial expense categories. We included the following seven items in the primary financing category: (1) tax effort, (2) taxes per capita, (3) intergovernmental revenue as a percent of total local revenue, (4) total debt per capita, (5) municipal capital spending per capita, (6) education expenses per capita, and (7) current operating expenses per capita. All other items are subtotals of expenses and are classified in the secondary financial category because they are part of the disaggregated current expenses.

Additionally, it should be noted that we have broken the data down in terms of whether the higher proportions are on the expense (the demand) side or on the revenue (the capacity) side. This is important because economic, social, and structural conditions affect directly the expense side of the municipality's operating statements and, in turn, the revenue financing means.

Note that the financial performance of Hartford, Stamford, and Boston has begun to reach the limits in terms of the primary revenue performance measures: in these cities, two out of four categories exceed 90 percent of the upper limit of the whole sample. Note also that only two cities—Hartford and Fresno—have primary expense measures above the 90 percent barrier. In combination, Hartford would appear to be the most extreme of all cities in the 66 cities sample. This is the negative dimension to be derived from the data in Table 7.2.

The positive dimension is that the revenue rates of 5 of the 11 cities are below the 90 percent barrier and that 9 of 11 cities fall below 90 percent in their primary expense items. Therefore, it is clear that most of these cities have revenue and expenditure options left before their outer limits as defined by our survey are reached. Finally, 5 of the 11 cities have secondary expense options with considerable flexibility. This encouraging conclusion is only somewhat offset by the expense rates of Hartford, Stamford, and Boston, which exceed 90 percent.

Finally, it will be worthwhile to note the variations in the economic, social, and structural conditions of these 11 cities. As we saw in Table 7.2, 6 cities (Buffalo, Hartford, Pittsburgh, Boston, Trenton, and Baltimore) of the 11 fall in the average to below-average private investment and income categories, and are also large dependent population, high population density cities. Another 3 cities

Table 7.2
Number of Financial Performance Variables (above 90 Percent) Approaching the Maximum Limit

City	Private Investment and Income	Dependent Population	Population Density	Primary Financial Performance Variables		Secondary Financial Performance Variables	Gross Total
				Expense	Revenue	Expense	
Buffalo	Below average	Large	High	0	1	0	1
Denver	High	Small	High	0	0	1	1
Stamford	Above average	Small	Low	0	3	1	4
Hartford	Below average	Large	High	1	2	2	5
Pittsburgh	Average	Large	High	0	0	0	0
Boston	Average	Large	High	0	2	1	3
Richmond	Below average	Large	Low	0	1	1	3
Trenton	Below average	Large	High	0	0	0	1
Atlanta	Below average	Large	Low	0	0	0	0
Baltimore	Average	Large	High	1	2	1	0
Fresno	Below average	Large	Low	0	0	1	3
Potential maximum				2	5	6	13

(Richmond, Atlanta, and Fresno) have average to below-average private investment and income conditions and either a large ratio of dependent populations or
high population densities. Only the remaining 2 cities (Stamford and Denver)
appear to be significantly out of character with the other 11 because of their
stronger economic conditions.

Thus, it may be concluded that in the most extended cases—Hartford,
Stamford, and Boston—only slightly more than one-third of the total financial
performance measures have reached the limits for the sample base. And even
among these cities, Stamford's generally favorable economic conditions and
growth potential must not be overlooked. Moreover, it is clear among all 11
cities that there is still some latitude for upward adjustment in other financing
sources, or downward adjustment in selected expense categories.

Another way to look at the proportions contained in Table 7.2 is the
number of times the individual tax and expense items fall at least 50 percent
below the maximum limits. Following the statistical procedures established
above, Table 7.3 provides this information.

The information contained in Table 7.3 is helpful in providing a more
complete understanding of the concept of limits. Note the specific pattern that
emerges: high-score cities in the 90 percent or above category score low in the
50 percent or below category—Hartford, Stamford, and Boston. Conversely,
cities that score low in the 90 percent or above category consistently score high
in the 50 percent or below category—most notably, Pittsburgh and Trenton.

The situations of Pittsburgh and Trenton need elaboration. Cities can and
sometimes do buck the financial trend that is strongly associated with their

Table 7.3
Number of Financial Performance Variables Below 50 Percent of the
Maximum Limit

| City | Primary Financial Performance Variables | | Secondary Financial Performance Variables | Gross Total |
	Expense	Revenue	Expense	
Buffalo	0	2	3	5
Denver	1	2	2	5
Stamford	0	1	2	3
Hartford	0	0	0	0
Pittsburgh	1	4	4	9
Boston	0	0	3	3
Richmond	0	0	3	3
Trenton	1	2	2	5
Atlanta	0	1	3	4
Baltimore	0	1	1	2
Fresno	0	3	4	7
Potential maximum	2	5	6	13

economic circumstances. Despite the fact that they are old industrialized cities, their tax, debt, and expense ratios have been managed or controlled. Clearly, this is the case with Trenton and Pittsburgh. These cities provide an excellent example of what may be described as a fundamental equilibrium between economic resources and financial performance, even as the advanced stages of industrialization are reached.

On the other hand, the cities of Atlanta, Fresno, and especially Denver, offer insight into growing cities that may be approaching their limits well before the advanced stages of industrialization have been reached. These cities appear to be younger variants of cities in the advanced stages, with their financial performance more in line with that of their older rather than their growing counterparts. Unquestionably, additional research needs to be undertaken, but these examples are highly suggestive of this concept.

Finally, we may turn our attention to the performance of four widely used nonfinancial variables. In order to gain a better perspective of the proportional magnitude of these variables among these 11 cities, we have prepared the frequency distributions shown in Table 7.4.

Three specific observations may be made:

Somewhat surprisingly, there is a relatively wide distribution among the 11 cities in terms of their minority ratios and population densities. Specifically, only 3 cities have minority ratios in excess of 80 percent of the maximum for the sample, and only 2 have densities above that ratio. The latter is interesting because much of the analysis up to this point has emphasized the causal relationship between population density and higher taxes, debt, and expenses. At first glance, the performance of these 11 cities seems to run counter to this finding. However, one must recognize the unusually great variances among the sample cities about the mean. Specifically, the mean value for population density is 4,869 persons per square mile, and the standard deviation is 3,386. Thus, a maximum value of 16,187 is more than

Table 7.4
Frequency Distribution of Four Nonfinancial Variables

Percent of Maximum Limit	Percent Minority Population	Percent pre-1939 Housing	Population Density	Manufacturing Capital Spending per Capita
90-100%	2	5	0	0
80-89	1	5	2	0
70-79	1	1	1	0
60-69	1	0	1	1
50-59	1	0	2	0
40-49	3	0	0	0
30-39	2	0	1	0
20-29	0	0	3	2
10-19	0	0	1	5
0-9	0	0	0	3

three standard deviations from the 66 cities mean. That 6 of 11 cities were well in excess of two standard deviations from the mean, and within 50 percent or close to such an extreme value, suggests that density does, indeed, make a difference.

The unusually high ratio of older housing—10 of 11 cities above 80 percent of the sample maximum—is a most striking characteristic, but it probably reflects the fact that these cities are in the older industrialized regions of the country. It does seem to suggest that this social condition variable can provide some insight into municipal financial performance.

The extraordinarily low manufacturing capital spending standings were consistent with our expectations; namely, the cost-effective investment environment in these cities has been severely weakened. Thus, manufacturing capital spending is simply taking place elsewhere. Note that 10 of the 11 cities have manufacturing capital spending standings that are at least no more than 29 percent of the maximum value.

The discussion to this point has provided insight into the extent to which the 66 cities are distributed around the means for the key Short List Variables. The widely held perception is that there are significant variances across municipal tax, debt, and expense rates. On the basis of this analysis of statistical dispersion, this does not seem to be the case. In reality, the vast majority of cities cluster around the aggregate means and there are few outliers—a conclusion that runs counter to expectations.

Nonetheless, to be meaningful as well as more rigorous, the concept of fiscal stress must necessarily take into account more than the Short List of Financial Variables. It must also reflect the underlying resources, the capacity of a city to support high tax, debt, or spending rates.

The methodology used earlier in this book classified cities into 16 homogeneous economic, social, and structural clusters and then determined the impact of these forces on municipal financial performance. Grouping the 66 cities into the 16 clusters provided a meaningful way of judging the compatibility of a city's underlying capacity with its financial performance. In other words, the 6 cities that are classified in the low population density, high private investment and income cluster are confronted with very similar external forces. Thus, the consistency, or inconsistency, of the municipal financial response provides insight into the extent to which the city's tax, debt, and expense rates are in rough equilibrium with the city's underlying resource capacity. It is in this sense that extreme and presumably unexplained variations in an individual city's financial performance relative to the cluster mean within the relatively homogeneous economic, social, and structural cluster may be an early sign that financial difficulty is, or has been, encountered. On the other hand, lower-than-expected municipal financial performance would certainly provide insight into a municipality with considerable underutilized resource capacity. Unquestionably, factors other than capacity—local preferences, for example—may influence municipal financial performance. These factors, however, cannot be quantified for statistical analysis. To assess the willingness of local citizens to support high taxes, expenses, and debt—as contrasted with what they are economically capable of supporting—one would have to examine local political and attitudinal factors.

In order to begin to develop a more complete understanding of the linkage between resource capacity and spending rates as well as to refine the concept of stress, we identified all the cities which had tax, debt, or expense performance greater than one standard deviation above the cluster mean. These are shown in Table 7.5.

A number of generalizations may be made about the cities classified as outliers in this table. Only 4 cities of the 66—Stamford, Boston, Hartford, and Atlanta—fall outside one standard deviation in terms of their tax, debt, and expense ratios within their relatively homogeneous resource capacity clusters. Eight additional cities—Denver, Bloomington, Seattle, Worcester, Duluth, Long Beach, Richmond, and Fresno—are outside the one standard deviation limit in two of the three key measures of financial performance. The conclusion is that, relative to the counterpart cities in their clusters, these tax, debt, and expense rates are not only high, but are most likely pushed near or beyond underlying capacity.

The 12 statistically outlying cities are scattered throughout the extreme variations in good and bad economic, social, and structural clusters. For the 3 old industrialized cities—Hartford, Boston, and Worcester—this may well imply fiscal stress. The 2 industrially maturing cities, Duluth and Seattle, are also out of line with their economically grouped counterparts. The remaining 7 cities were classified as young growing cities. Because of their stronger economic base, their high expenses, taxes, and debt may not be a sign of imminent stress. Rather, these patterns may suggest that a financial pattern has been established and as the cities age, or experience an economic downturn, fiscal stress is likely to result.

Finally, it should not be minimized that 54 cities—the vast majority—appear to have maintained their tax, debt, and expense ratios in line with underlying resources capacity. At the least, it may be argued that their tax, debt, and expense rates are relatively close to the individual cluster means. This indicates rather clearly a generally consistent response to homogeneous external economic, social, and structural forces.

We may now attempt to summarize our position on financial limits.

Summary

The concept of limits provides, at best, a relative barrier which, as cities begin to approach it, indicates that a number of expense and revenue trade-off options are greatly diminished, and that should expenditure rates continue to outpace

Table 7.5
Fiscal Stress: Cities with Taxing, Debt, and Spending Rates Greater than One Standard Deviation from the Means of Their Economic Clusters

Cluster	Number of Cities in Cluster	Cities with Tax Performance Greater than One Standard Deviation above Cluster Mean	Cities with Debt Performance Greater than One Standard Deviation above Cluster Mean	Cities with Expense Performance Greater than One Standard Deviation above Cluster Mean
High private investment and income:				
Large dependent population	2		(Insufficient data in cluster)	
Small dependent population	7	Denver	Bloomington Baton Rouge	Denver
High population density	3		(Insufficient data in cluster)	
Low population density	6	Bloomington	Baton Rouge	Bloomington
Above-average private investment and income:				
Large dependent population	6	Evanston Stamford	Kansas City Stamford	Stamford
Small dependent population	6		Seattle Stamford	Seattle
High population density	6	Evanston Stamford		Stamford
Low population density	6			
Average private investment and income:				
Large dependent population	13	Boston	Louisville Boston	Pasadena Dayton Boston
Small dependent population	13	Cambridge Worcester	Eugene Wichita	Duluth Worcester Minneapolis

Table 7.5 continued

Cluster	Number of Cities in Cluster	Cities with Tax Performance Greater than One Standard Deviation above Cluster Mean	Cities with Debt Performance Greater than One Standard Deviation above Cluster Mean	Cities with Expense Performance Greater than One Standard Deviation above Cluster Mean
High population density	11	Cambridge Boston	Louisville Minneapolis Boston Eugene Duluth Wichita	Pasadena Dayton Boston Duluth Worcester
Low population density	15	Worcester		
Below-average private investment and income:				
Large dependent population	14	New Haven Hartford Richmond	Hartford Richmond Atlanta	Hartford
Small dependent population	5	Long Beach Hartford		Long Beach Hartford Fresno Tampa Atlanta
High population density	5	Fresno Richmond Atlanta	Hartford Richmond Atlanta	
Low population density	14			

revenue capacity, financial disequilibrium would result. The reader should bear in mind, however, that qualitative judgments about services are beyond the scope of this study. Thus, while expenditure cuts may be necessary to prevent financial disequilibrium, such cuts may—although not necessarily—affect the quality of services.

The concept of limits, whether defined in terms of deviations from the overall mean for all 66 cities or in terms of the 16 homogeneous clusters, appears to be a reasonably worthwhile statistical discriminator between cities that have quite similar, or dissimilar, responses to external forces.

Furthermore, it seems clear that of the 66 municipalities analyzed only slightly more than 15 percent of the cities appear to be approaching, or have approached, their financial limits. This conclusion runs counter to the widely held perception that many of our medium-to-large cities are confronted with serious financial problems, and for that matter must have substantial infusions of external funds to survive financially.

Ultimately, much more empirical work needs to be undertaken on the subject of municipal fiscal stress. Specifically, we need to know more about precisely where the "limit barrier" begins and how it can be more accurately identified statistically. This poses a complex research problem for a number of reasons. First, the empirical measurement of a municipality's financial limits is a function of the number of cities in the study—in our case, 66. Accordingly, one may legitimately ask whether those cities constitute the "proper set" whose cumulative expense and revenue experience should determine the limit. Second, as economic growth takes place, the outer boundaries are expanded, thus providing additional room for expanding municipal options. But as growth declines, the limits will most certainly be reached at a much faster rate. This implies that the concept of limits must ultimately be judged as a dynamic one.

Finally, the geographical mix of the stressed cities is also of interest. It is shown in Table 7.6. Despite the fact that we believe the resource capacity approach (that is, measuring a city's financial performance against cities in similar economic circumstances) represents a stronger analytical tool than measuring a city against all others in the data base, it is interesting to note the general level of consistency, whichever technique is used. The preponderance of Northeastern cities experiencing fiscal stress was expected, and in fact was identified throughout the analysis. The fiscal performance of some Western and Southern cities gives rise to the view that they may well be "younger variants" of their Northeastern counterparts. It is a tentative conclusion, but it suggests that some cities may respond in a financial manner characteristic of old industrialized cities, even though they have not yet reached that stage.

On the basis of this analysis, it is reasonable to conclude that the most financially pressed cities are in the industrially mature Northeast: 6 of the 11 analyzed were considered to be close to their limits in a number of their key expense, debt, and revenue categories. There is still another dimension to the concept of limits, and this pertains to the 55 cities whose expense and revenue

Table 7.6
Geographical Regions of Fiscally Stressed Cities

	Number of Cities Classified as Stressed in Terms of 66 Cities Means	Number of Cities Classified as Stressed in Terms of Cluster Means	Total Sample
Northeast	6	4	12
South	3	2	18
Southwest	0	0	8
Midwest	0	2	11
High Plains	0	0	5
West	2	4	12
Total	11	12	66

measures fall short of the situations specifically discussed in this section. For these cities, there are obviously quite a few discretionary trade-offs available before limits are approached. The key seems to be to understand and to anticipate the dynamics that push a city toward its limits.

Looking backward in our analyses, it appears that nearly all of the 66 municipalities have managed to balance financial capacity (tax revenue, intergovernmental transfers, and debt) quite satisfactorily against the demands of local expenditures. Even among many of the cities with stagnant or declining population and below-average private investment and income, the allocation of local resources and intergovernmental transfers to meet priority service demands has apparently not pushed them even close to the outer limits. Generally speaking, the exceptions to this encouraging performance are few, and they are concentrated among older Northeastern cities with large dependent populations and high population densities.

In conclusion, the definition and measurement of municipal fiscal stress will undoubtedly be refined in the years ahead. In the interim, this analysis can provide a framework for examining municipal fiscal stress in financial terms and for assessing the dynamic linkages between nonfinancial conditions and municipal financial performance.

Appendix A
Correlation Matrix of Economic Base Variables and Financial Performance Indicators

In order to develop a more complete understanding of the manner in which economic, social, structural, and municipal financial performance variables interact, we calculated a correlation matrix for 11 socio-economic variables and 12 financial variables. The correlation matrix for the 66 cities across these variables is shown in Table A.1.

The 23 variables are identified by the following numbers:

Variable Number	*Description*
1	Percentage change in population 1960-75
2	Population density
3	Minority population ratio
4	Median family income
5	Percentage of families below low-income level
6	Ratio of manufacturing employment, 1970
7	Unemployment rate
8	Percent single-family housing
9	Ratio pre-1939 housing stock
10	Private capital spending, 1970
11	Private capital spending per capita
12	Ratio of local taxes to personal income
13	Local taxes per capita
14	Intergovernmental revenue as a percent of total local revenue
15	Total debt per capita
16	Interest per capita
17	Municipal capital spending per capita, five-year average, 1971-75
18	Fire expenses per capita
19	Education expenses per capita
20	Health expenses per capita
21	Welfare expenses per capita
22	Ratio of city full-time-equivalent employment to total local employment
23	Average city employee annual income

Table A.1
Correlation Matrix

	1)	2)	3)	4)	5)	6)	7)	8)	9)	10)	11)	12)	13)	14)	15)	16)	17)	18)	19)	20)	21)	22)
1)	1.00																					
2)	-.31																					
3)	-.16	.02																				
4)	.15	.11	-.54																			
5)	-.14	-.08	.79	-.84																		
6)	-.11	.30	.02	.18	-.16																	
7)	-.18	.14	.06	-.27	.21	.10																
8)	.26	-.71	.10	-.15	.10	-.32	.01															
9)	-.20	.51	-.15	.17	-.23	.46	-.03	-.62														
10)	-.07	.21	.12	-.02	.04	.50	.13	-.14	.19													
11)	.02	.08	.14	.04	.02	.43	.10	.06	.07	.45												
12)	-.25	.57	.09	.09	-.02	.33	-.02	-.74	.48	.17	.05											
13)	-.21	.54	-.06	.37	-.24	.27	-.12	-.71	.46	.11	.05	.91										
14)	-.05	.17	.10	-.15	.10	.16	.16	-.09	.17	.33	-.05	-.02	-.13									
15)	.06	.03	.05	.13	-.01	.08	-.13	-.25	.08	.12	-.04	.37	.41	-.07								
16)	.08	.09	.16	.20	.01	.12	-.18	-.21	.07	.07	.08	.36	.46	-.06	.77							
17)	-.17	.27	.08	.07	.00	.31	-.04	-.53	.30	.19	-.05	.52	.52	.31	.58	.54						
18)	-.35	.59	.13	-.13	.15	.29	.23	-.72	.46	.03	-.10	.65	.58	.26	.18	.19	.57					
19)	-.03	.13	-.20	.47	-.37	.06	-.03	-.25	.19	-.01	-.07	.38	.49	.16	.30	.26	.32	.25				
20)	-.17	.32	.14	.14	-.07	.16	-.04	-.28	.25	.21	-.02	.50	.57	.02	.18	.31	.29	.39	.10			
21)	-.11	.23	.27	-.04	.12	.17	-.10	-.36	.21	.06	-.08	.58	.52	.16	.37	.35	.55	.44	.25	.58		
22)	-.26	.56	.22	-.21	.23	.26	.04	-.63	.37	.12	-.07	.65	.53	.33	.31	.27	.73	.75	.11	.38	.55	
23)	-.04	.33	-.24	.54	-.44	.21	.19	-.25	.26	.12	.09	.36	.45	-.02	.03	.05	.03	.23	.63	.28	.07	-.01

A careful analysis of the correlation coefficients contained in the Table A.1 matrix yields a great deal of significant information about the manner in which social, economic, structural, and financial variables interact across the 66 cities. Before we review this information, a very brief comment will be helpful in interpreting the specific r's (coefficients of correlation) in the matrix. The variables are listed across the columns and down the rows. Each cell contains the correlation coefficient (the r) that describes the degree of association between the two variables under consideration. The limits of perfect association are +1.00 to −1.00, while a random association is described by an r equal to or approaching 0. Note that in the first cell, variable 1 correlated against itself equals 1.00. By contrast, a weak correlation can be found in the cell for variable 1 (column 1) and variable 10 (row 10) − $r = .07$, thus indicating a mildly negative but nearly random relationship between changes in population and the unemployment rate. In order to develop a shorthand understanding of these r's, statisticians usually square the correlation coefficient. This ratio—R^2—represents the ratio of the variance explained by one variable with respect to the total variance in the other variable. In the example above, the R^2 amounts to .0049, suggesting that less than one-hundredth of one percent in the changes in the unemployment rate among the 66 cities can be explained by changes in population.

There are a number of specific conclusions that can be derived from the various coefficients shown in the matrix. These are discussed in terms of the three relevant subsets contained in the matrix.

The Socio-Economic Variable
Portion of the Matrix

Only 7 of the total 54 social, economic, and structural variables show coefficients of .50 or more ($R^2 = .25$) Thus, in 83 percent of the cases, the degree of co-variation is so weak as to be statistically insignificant or to follow a random pattern. In more than one-half of the significant cases, the degree of interdependence is implicit—e.g., variables that measure median family income and families below the low-income level, which are by definition interrelated.

The change in population 1960-75 variable is statistically insignificant in its behavior for *all* the other ten social, economic, and structural variables. This tells us clearly that changes in population are an incredibly poor descriptive measure across samples of cities that are obviously experiencing differences in their economic growth rates and responding with significant variations in their municipal expenditure demands.

An interesting and moderately strong, but inverse, correlation appears to exist for a city's population density and the percentage of single-family units ($r = −.71$), as well as for population density and the ratio of pre-1939 housing stock ($r = -.51$). Both of these relationships are expected and are entirely consistent with the real-world realities determined by the size of the city.

The Financial Variable Portion
of the Matrix

Of the 55 correlation coefficients among the financial variables, 21 relationships—38 percent—may be classified as being moderately to highly significant. Given the highly interactive nature of a municipality's operating account, this is not especially surprising. Alternatively, it is somewhat surprising to note that 62 percent of the variables appear to be responding to other factors.

This conclusion notwithstanding, it is interesting to note that the intergovernmental transfer variable shows absolutely no degree of statistical association with any of the 11 other financial variables. The highest r amounts to .33 and is for the ratio of FTE municipal workers to total employment—at best a confusing degree of co-association.

As expected, variances in tax variables are closely associated with variances in the current and capital expenditure variables. This is the case with both tax-performance measures.

The Socio-Economic and Financial
Variable Portion of the Matrix

Among the 132 correlation coefficients contained in the social, economic, structural, and financial variable matrix, only 9 variables showed coefficients of .50 or greater, implying that 93 percent of the paired variables have at best only a weak statistical relationship or more likely a random one. This conclusion, unquestionably, is reminding us of how difficult it is to generalize any kind of meaningful cause and effect relationship when social, economic, and structural conditions and municipal financial performance are indiscriminately mixed.

The nine variables in which there was a relatively strong degree of statistical association were concentrated in two financial areas. Specifically, variations in population densities appear to be correlated with variances in the ratio of taxes to income (+.57), taxes per capita (+.54), fire expenses per capita (+.59), and the ratio of FTE to total employment (+.56). The second area where significant associations are present is the variance between the percentage of single-family housing units and the following five financial variables: ratio of taxes to income (+.74), taxes per capita (+.71), municipal capital spending per capita (+.53), fire expenses per capita (+.72), and the ratio of FTE to total employment (+.63).

Overall, the correlation ratios appear to be sufficiently weak so as to give considerable support to the viewpoint that changes in social, economic, and structural conditions are not generally valid statistical indicators of municipal financial performance. In some specific cases—e.g., population change and unemployment rate—the relationship can only be described as random. Yet, there are two noteworthy exceptions—population density and single-family housing—and these should be accorded greater attention by researchers and policymakers alike. The limited degree of statistical association among many of the financial variables themselves is also noteworthy, suggesting that there are many different municipal forces that influence changes in tax, debt, and expense variables. Again, we are reminded of the necessity for more detailed and comprehensive analysis of factors affecting municipal financial conditions.

It should be very clear from the foregoing comments that until and unless changes in social, economic, and structural conditions are systematically organized into some kind of analytical framework, it will be virtually impossible to determine the impact on the municipal financial operating statement.

Appendix B
The 66 Cities

1. Mobile AL
2. Montgomery AL
3. Phoenix AZ
4. Tempe AZ
5. Tucson AZ
6. Little Rock AR
7. Daly City CA
8. Fresno CA
9. Long Beach CA
10. Pasadena CA
11. Denver CO
12. Pueblo CO
13. Bridgeport CT
14. Hartford CT
15. New Haven CT
16. Stamford CT
17. Hollywood FL
18. Jacksonville FL
19. St. Petersburg FL
20. Tampa FL
21. West Palm Beach FL
22. Atlanta GA
23. Savannah GA
24. Decatur IL
25. Evanston IL
26. Indianapolis IN
27. Topeka KS
28. Wichita KS
29. Louisville KY
30. Baton Rouge LA
31. New Orleans LA
32. Baltimore MD
33. Boston MA
34. Cambridge MA
35. Springfield MA
36. Worcester MA
37. Grand Rapids MI
38. Bloomington MN
39. Duluth MN
40. Minneapolis MN
41. Rochester MN
42. Jackson MS
43. Kansas City MO
44. Lincoln NB
45. Omaha NB
46. Trenton NJ
47. Albuquerque NM
48. Buffalo NY
49. Syracuse NY
50. Greensboro NC
51. Dayton OH
52. Eugene OR
53. Pittsburgh PA
54. Amarillo TX
55. Austin TX
56. Forth Worth TX
57. Galveston TX
58. Irving TX
59. Port Arthur TX
60. San Angelo TX
61. Salt Lake City UT
62. Richmond VA
63. Seattle WA
64. Spokane WA
65. Madison WI
66. Milwaukee WI

Appendix C
Map Showing
Geographic
Distribution of the 66
Cities

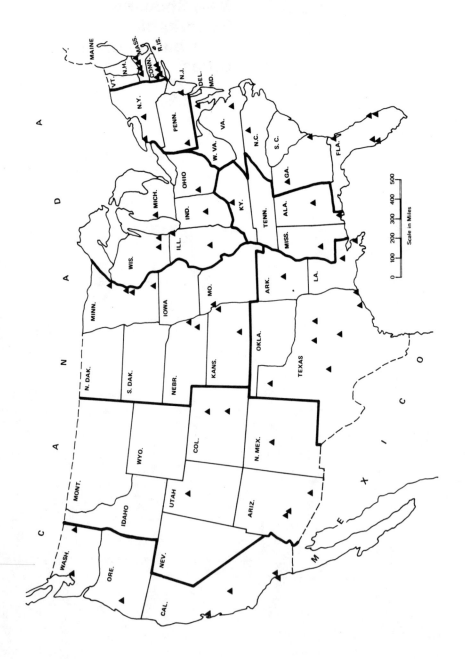

Appendix D
Data Sources for the
66 Cities Study

1. U.S. Department of Commerce, Bureau of the Census

   City Government Finances in 1974-75 (GF75 #4)

   City Government Finances in 1975-76 (GF76 #4)

   City Government Finances in 1969-70 (GF70 #4)

   City Government Finances in 1970-71 (GF71 #4)

   Computer magtapes with backup detail for the above publications for FY 1969-70, 1970-71, 1974-75, 1975-76.

2. U.S. Department of Commerce, Bureau of the Census

   Survey of Local School Districts: School Systems (Form OMD #41 - P2735) for individual municipalities

   Data for revenues, expenditures, and debt of independent and county dependent school districts were obtained from this source. Where the school district boundaries were not coterminous with the city boundaries, the school data were multiplied by the percentage of the school district which served the city.

3. Individual municipality audit reports for FY 1970 and FY 1975

   Balance sheet data on liabilities, cash, pension liability, and fixed assets were aggregated from the audit reports. Information on assessments, tax rates, maturity of debt, direct and overlapping debt, and property tax collections were taken from the statistical sections of the audit reports. General fund surplus, expenditures, and budgeted and actual revenues were from this source.

4. Moody's Municipal Manual for FY 1970 and FY 1975

   Moody's ratings were obtained from this publication. In addition, data on property tax and assessments which were not available in the audit reports were obtained from this source. Standard and Poor's bond rating pamphlet was used to obtain S&P ratings.

5. Census of Government, 1972

   Information on the sales value of taxable property, effective tax rates, and total local government debt by county was obtained from this set of publications.

6. U.S. Department of Commerce, Bureau of the Census
   City and County Data Book, 1977
   City and County Data Book, 1972
   City and County Data Book, 1952
   Current Population Reports, series P-25, May 1977
   1972 Census of Manufacturers

Appendix E
Cross-Reference to the 66 Cities as They Appear in the Text

Albuquerque NM, 9, 58, 65, 67, 112, 113, 115, 117, 118, 145

Amarillo TX, 9, 57, 65, 67, 102, 104, 106, 108, 109, 145

Atlanta GA, 9, 12, 13, 14, 15, 58, 65, 67, 113, 114, 117, 118, 127, 128, 130, 131, 132, 134, 136, 145

Austin TX, 9, 58, 65, 67, 113, 115, 117, 118, 145

Baltimore MD, 7, 9, 10, 16, 17, 18, 20, 58, 60, 65, 67, 101, 103, 105, 108, 109, 121, 126, 127, 128, 129, 130, 131, 145

Baton Rouge LA, 9, 15, 57, 65, 67, 80, 81, 83, 85, 87, 119, 121, 135, 145

Bloomington MN, 9, 14, 15, 57, 65, 67, 80, 81, 83, 85, 87, 89, 96, 119, 121, 134, 135, 145

Boston MA, 9, 10, 14, 15, 58, 60, 65, 67, 101, 103, 105, 108, 127, 128, 129, 130, 131, 134, 135, 136, 145

Bridgeport CT, 9, 10, 58, 59, 65, 67, 101, 103, 104, 105, 108, 145

Buffalo NY, 9, 10, 16, 17, 18, 58, 60, 65, 67, 112, 113, 114, 116, 118, 121, 126, 127, 128, 129, 130, 131, 145

Cambridge MA, 9, 10, 15, 58, 59, 65, 67, 101, 104, 105, 108, 135, 136, 145

Daly City CA, 9, 57, 65, 67, 90, 92, 93, 97, 145

Dayton OH, 9, 10, 15, 57, 60, 65, 67, 101, 103, 105, 108, 135, 136, 145

Decatur IL, 9, 57, 65, 67, 90, 91, 94, 95, 100, 145

Denver CO, 9, 12, 13, 14, 15, 57, 65, 67, 80, 81, 83, 84, 86, 87, 89, 96, 97, 119, 127, 128, 130, 131, 132, 134, 135, 145

Duluth MN, 9, 10, 14, 15, 57, 60, 65, 67, 101, 104, 106, 108, 134, 135, 136, 145

Eugene OR, 9, 15, 57, 65, 67, 102, 104, 106, 108, 135, 136, 145

Evanston IL, 9, 15, 57, 65, 67, 90, 91, 93, 100, 135, 145

Fort Worth TX, 9, 16, 17, 18, 57, 65, 67, 90, 92, 94, 98, 145

Fresno CA, 9, 14, 15, 58, 65, 67, 113, 114, 117, 118, 121, 126, 127, 128, 129, 130, 131, 132, 134, 136, 145

Galveston TX, 9, 58, 65, 67, 113, 114, 117, 118, 145

Grand Rapids MI, 9, 57, 65, 67, 90, 91, 93, 100, 145

Greensboro NC, 9, 57, 65, 67, 101, 104, 106, 108, 145

Hartford CT, 9, 10, 14, 15, 58, 59, 65, 67, 112, 113, 114, 116, 118, 121 126, 127, 128, 129, 130, 131, 134, 136, 145

Hollywood FL, 9, 57, 65, 67, 80, 81, 83, 85, 87, 119, 121, 145

Indianapolis IN, 9, 16, 17, 18, 57, 65, 67, 80, 81, 82, 85, 87, 121, 145

Irving TX, 9, 57, 65, 67, 80, 81, 83, 85, 87, 119, 121, 145

Jackson MS, 9, 58, 65, 67, 112, 113, 114, 117, 118, 145

Jacksonville FL, 9, 16, 17, 18, 57, 65, 67, 80, 81, 82, 85, 87, 121, 145

Kansas City MO 9, 15, 57, 65, 67, 90, 91, 94, 135, 145

Lincoln NB, 9, 57, 65, 67, 101, 104, 106, 108, 145

Little Rock AR, 9, 57, 65, 67, 101, 104, 106, 108, 145

About the Authors

James M. Howell, Senior Vice President and chief economist of The First National Bank of Boston, undertook his undergraduate training at Texas A&M University and graduate training in economics at Tulane University. Since receiving the Ph.D. in 1963, he has been a faculty member of The George Washington University, The University of Maryland, and Tulane University.

From 1962 through 1970, Dr. Howell held several positions with the Federal Government, including economic advisor to the Assistant Secretary of Commerce for Economic Affairs and Economist to the Board of Governors of the Federal Reserve System. During this period, he was also an economic advisor to the government of Chile.

Dr. Howell has served in an advisory capacity on urban economic development to a number of government agencies and is currently Chairman of the Council for Northeast Economic Action, which conducts research and undertakes projects involving urban revitalization.

Charles F. Stamm, a principal of Touche Ross & Co., San Francisco, California, received the bachelor's degree in chemical engineering from Georgia Institute of Technology and the master's degree in business administration from New York University. Before joining Touche Ross & Co., Mr. Stamm worked as manager for Genesco and as production engineer for Colgate-Palmolive Company.

Mr. Stamm has written a number of journal articles and has contributed to the *AMA Management Handbook* for the American Management Associations. Currently, Mr. Stamm is a member of the Institute of Management Consultants and is a certified management consultant.